I'm delighted to recommend this enjoyable and edifying book.
Kim and Bruce Money offer wise parenting advice for all ages as well
as specific solutions to everyday family problems.
—Dr. Stephen R. Covey

Sincerely,
Bruce + Kim Money

Creating a Functional Family in a Dysfunctional World

Kimberly K. Money, LISW
R. Bruce Money, PhD

Taylor Publishing Company
Dallas, Texas

Designed by David Timmons

Published by Taylor Publishing Company
1550 West Mockingbird Lane
Dallas, Texas 75235
www.taylorpub.com

Library of Congress Cataloging-in-Publication Data:

Money, Kimberly K.
        Creating a functional family in a dysfunctional world / Kimberly K. Money,
R. Bruce Money.
            p   cm.
        Includes bibliographical references.
        ISBN 0-87833-238-3
        1. Child rearing. 2. Parent and child. I. Money, R. Bruce (Richard Bruce) II. Title.
HQ769.M563   1999
649'.1—dc21   99-32896
                                                                                       CIP

10 9   8   7   6   5   4   3   2   1
Printed in the United States of America

To our parents, who gave us life and all the good things it holds,
and to our children,
Kristy, Ryan, McKay, twins Tanner and Aubrey, and Madison,
who help us realize the difference between that which is really important
and that which is not.

Contents

Acknowledgments   viii

Introduction   ix

1   *A Democratic Republic in the Family Structure*   1

2   *Why Children Misbehave*   21

3   *Your Marriage Matters in Parenting*   40

4   *Birth Order and Behavior*   53

5   *Encouraging Children*   65

6   *Empowering Children Through Reflective Listening*   79

7   *Problem Ownership and Resolution*   90

8   *Consequences that Create Responsibility*   106

9   *Consequences for Specific Challenges*   127

10   *The Overdiagnosed Attention Deficit Disorder*   144

11   *Holding Family Meetings*   158

12   *Blended Families: Step-Success*   170

     Conclusion   182

     Index   188

Acknowledgments

We would like to thank:

Grandma Klecker, who watched the twins when needed during the early phases of the manuscript.

Our editor, Camille Cline at Taylor Publishing, who gave us some fabulous ideas and brought this book from our home to yours.

Pat Berman at the *State* newspaper in Columbia, South Carolina, who took an interest in what we had to say and gave it the voice of the press.

Sally Davis, whose early help in editing got us off to a good start.

The many parents, friends, educators, colleagues, clients, physicians, and mental health professionals who encouraged us to write this book.

Parenting in Our Turbulent Times

F ew would question that the job of parenting is tough and getting tougher. In an *American Demographics* magazine survey, 78 percent of people aged 30 to 39 and 90 percent of those aged 50 to 64 agree that it is more difficult to be a parent now than twenty or thirty years ago. Parents today are raising children in an environment increasingly hostile to a stable family life. The *Houston Chronicle* reports that by the day of high school graduation, 80 percent of teens have tried alcohol and the average child has viewed 200,000 acts of violence on television. Sixty-four percent of inner-city youths believe that having a child out of wedlock is acceptable, and only half of all tenth-grade girls think it is a bad idea. A *Who's Who in American High Schools* survey found that 56 percent of top female high school students had been sexually assaulted and 17 percent had attempted suicide.

Other demographic trends discourage traditional family structure. The number of 17-year-olds who live in families in which the father works, the mother stays home, and all the children were born after the parents' only marriage fell steadily this century to only 5 percent in 1997. The number of women who work full time who have children younger than six increased 30 percent from 1970 to 1995.

Single-parent families have risen from 11 percent to 25 percent in the past twenty years. Half of all marriages end in divorce. A University of Michigan study recently showed that children of divorce are twice as likely to become violent during spousal arguments.

Many would agree that at least some of the blame for these and other disturbing trends can be traced to a breakdown of the family structure and to poor parenting skills. Despite the troubles in his own family life, President Bill Clinton has publicly stressed the importance of parenting. He remarked in an interview, "I think that parenting is the most important job in this society and the one that has been neglected the most." Few world or local leaders would deny that parenting is critical to the well-being of a nation or a community. As former First Lady Barbara Bush stated, "What happens in the White House is not nearly as important as what happens in your house." A nation of dysfunctional families is a dysfunctional nation. The skill of parenting hasn't been effectively woven into the collective consciousness of society. We train and license people for many important functions of society, including doctors, teachers, and day-care workers. Even pets are licensed! Yet parents, the individuals most responsible for rearing the world's children, rarely undergo any training. They are left to parent as they were parented, for better or for worse.

An unbalanced system of autocratic parenting requires a superior-inferior relationship, the opposite of the basis for democracy. America's founding fathers purported that "all men are created equal." Although not stated nor even implied at that time in history, the saying applies nowadays to women and children, as well as minorities. Autocratic parenting styles regaining popularity today are rightly under attack for their imposition on children's fundamental rights as citizens of a democracy. Children of today rebel against autocracy, just as their parents did, but in different, much more dangerous forms. Instead of public demonstrations such as marching with banners, they now wage a more private, personal rebellion through self-destructive abuse of drugs and alcohol, eating disorders, and acts of violence toward others and themselves. Children use such means to escape their perceived inappropriate use of power and control.

How did your parents raise you? Their methods probably bring back many pleasant as well as unpleasant memories. Perhaps you remember an authoritarian parent who severely disciplined you, which you have never forgotten. You probably laugh now with siblings or friends about such incident. ("Remember the time I did … and Dad did ….") You didn't laugh at the time though, or, if too severe a punishment, you don't even laugh now. Were you the "difficult child," or "Mommy's little angel"? Again, these memories might bring pain or smiles, depending on the situation. We are amazed at how vivid these memories are when siblings in our own families of origin get together. These memories from childhood influence parents raising their own children.

Research shows that relationships between siblings change very little; in fact, relationships in later years between parents and children generally change very little as well. That is why we want to emphasize in this book that the story of your future relationships with your children is being written right now. While few would argue that it is never too late to change a relationship, those same few would agree that change is more difficult the older we get. Decide now that your own children's memories of their formative years in your home will be positive ones.

Parental roles have changed drastically in the last few decades. Think of how your parents or grandparents were raised. Early twentieth-century parenting styles were usually autocratic and controlling. The well-known saying "Children should be seen and not heard" was not only a saying back then but the way children were raised. "Reading and writing and 'rithmatic, taught to the tune of a hickory stick." As this line from the folk song "School Days" goes, corporal punishment was the norm in school and at home for children who stepped out of line, which made for a more disciplined student body and child populace in general. Today, many raised in that era long for the "good ol' days" of order that prevailed in schools and communities. That is what seems to be the positive side. The dark side was the lack of a formalized system to protect children from emotional and physical abuse. Whether actual abuse was as rampant then as it is today is a subject of well-placed debate, although reported child abuse is now undoubtedly at an all-time high. Reported cases of child abuse and neglect in the United States rose from 606,000 in 1978 to more than 3 million in 1996.

Parenting through the years has been a learn-as-you-go process, with little formalized training available, except for professionals such as family counselors, psychologists, or clergy. Unfortunately, seeking professional help for a problem often comes late in the process—an attempt to fix what is broken rather than prevent a breakdown in the first place. In the past, mainly the wealthy or those who felt a therapist was a status symbol ("Well, *my* therapist said...") sought mental therapy. Also, psychiatric patients were sometimes labeled "disturbed" or branded with some other such stigma. Left with little or no resources, parents in the earlier decades became extremely autocratic just to cope, seeing no other alternative. As a result, although some children responded well to the discipline of the day, many became sullen and withdrawn with little or no self-esteem.

Midcentury changes in the demographics of the United States affected the way parents and children viewed themselves in home and society. Women entering the workforce in great numbers during World War II developed an increased sense of power and independence as wage-earning members of society. Although many women returned to homemaking after the war, creating the baby boom, many continued holding full-time or part-time positions in the workforce. This phenomenon, combined with the women's movement of the 1960s, changed the way parents and children saw their roles in society and at home. Children rebelled against the autocratic style of their parents. "Never trust anyone over thirty" was as much a comment about parental roles as it was about authority figures at school or work. Flower children in the late 1960s felt free to roam and do as they pleased as the hippie movement became an icon of American culture of that decade.

When these flower children had children of their own, many were determined to break the mold of their parents' philosophy of parenting, casting aside the autocratic and controlling methods with which they were raised. However, as the debate goes, they may have cast them too far, with permissiveness and rule-free environments becoming the norm in many homes during the 1970s and 1980s. Because the balance of power had shifted dramatically toward children in the 1960s, the children born in that era continued the shift by bestowing upon their own children many rights and privileges that they never had themselves. Children with more rights bestowed upon them by well-meaning parents brought new parenting challenges that sowed the permissive seeds of many of the issues parents deal with today.

In many homes of the 1980s and 1990s, the children, not the parents, have dictated home rules and structure. Without reasonable limits, these children tend to feel they are entitled to maximum rights with minimum responsibility. Children often feel exempt from the consequences of their negative behaviors and are not willing to conform to what they perceive as arbitrary rules of their parents.

Because of these children's increasing resentments, many parents are tempted to retreat to autocratic parenting styles of the past. We see the parenting pendulum begin to swing back, as many trends do without a better alternative. This would require parents to again adopt a form of tyranny, which creates rebellion. No doubt, violence on school campuses could be lessened if children had a healthy balance of rules along with trust and respect within their own homes. As the philosophy of the Boy Scouts goes, "It is easier to build boys than to repair men."

Recently a friend of ours commented that he was listening to a popular radio show that featured a prominent local psychologist. After describing parenting styles in their extreme forms, both autocratic and permissive, the psychologist argued that both styles are destructive and create dysfunctional families. Her opinion was that our society's only hope is for parents to learn democratic parenting. Many callers began phoning in to find out where to learn democratic parenting to build children's self-esteem, promote responsibility, and increase respect for all family members, which is the reason we wrote this book. While no book or authors can guarantee a

100 percent success rate for their formula, in these chapters, we have tried to equip readers with the skills necessary to head a democratically functional household.

In the twenty-first century, parents must find a balance between autocracy and permissiveness to avoid the destructive cycles of today and the past. The key to this is creating a functioning democratic republic in the home. The reason history repeats itself, as the saying goes, is that nobody was listening the first time.

Authors' note:

We've done everything together in fifteen years of marriage—supported each other through several graduate degrees, cared for sick children, and enjoyed sunsets. So, too, was this book a joint effort. We wrote it together, with specific examples related from both our professional and personal experiences: Kimberly with her therapy practice and teaching professional seminars; Bruce in his work with youth groups, such as the Boy Scouts and coaching, and with students as a professor; and, of course, our family of six children.

A final note: All the names and identifying details in the examples have been changed.

One

A Democratic Republic in the Family Structure

lthough U.S. society is based on what are commonly called democratic principles, apparently most families are not. A recent *New York Times* poll asked parents to rate their style of parenting. About 50 percent reported their style as autocratic, 48 percent responded "permissive," and only 2 percent claimed to be running a democratic family. Granted, what some parents call democratic others may call permissive, which hearkens back to the way we were raised. Although semantic differences may partially account for the low score on democratic styles, the poll might explain some problems in our homes and in society that result from the extremes of autocratic versus permissive rule. Autocratic parenting means that the parent calls the shots. Although the literal translation of *autocracy* is "self-rule," it is the parent who rules—"what I say goes"—rather than the "self" of the child. It is similar to a monarchy—a king or queen, or worse, a tyrant, decides who does what when and the consequences for disobedience are severe: imprisonment or even execution. Some societies, such as those in many Islamic countries, are run this way with orderly results, but most people living in Western countries prefer individual freedoms. At the other extreme, the permissive parent allows anarchy (literally, "anti-government") in the home. There is no punishment for laws broken because there are no laws. Except for those extremists who assassinate heads of state, which started World War I, most people agree that permissiveness, at the far end of the spectrum, is no way to run either a society or a home. Although perhaps better described as anarchic than permissive, Bosnia, Croatia, and some newly independent regions of the former Yugoslavia might be characterized by the chaos of lawlessness.

Countless poems, novels and operas have been written about the struggle in society for freedom, which is reflected in the daily parenting battles at home. We're not saying Victor Hugo had parenting in mind when he reported the effect of the French Revolution in *Les Miserables,* but subtle parenting undercurrents do exist. It should also be noted that the United States is not governed by *democracy,* in the literal sense of the word, which translates from the Greek *damos,* "people," and *kratia,* "rule." Rather, the United States is actually a democratic republic in which officials elected by the people enact legislation and laws that are enforced by police vested with the power of the people to keep order for all. Parents are not exactly presidents, senators, nor police officers, but in a sense, they are elected or even appointed in that they are charged with the responsibility of raising kids who become responsible adults contributing to, not detracting from, the quality of life for society in general.

Of course, without laws and rules in society, chaos and eventual decay from within is certain, as the case has been in many great empires throughout history. Even though all parents have an obligation to train their children to observe order in society and in the home, the extremes of permissive and autocratic methods manifest themselves in children who have extreme difficulty accepting order, who have little respect for others, and who are excessively concerned with their own rights.

Training for the World's Most Important Job

It is difficult to believe that the vital skill of child rearing hasn't been more effectively woven into the collective parenting consciousness of our society. Parents, the individuals most responsible for rearing the world's children, are not required to undergo any formal training. Of course, enacting or implementing such training could not be done easily or inexpensively. Would there be state or federal standards for parenting? In cases of extreme child abuse or neglect, some people think that parenting rights (biologically or otherwise) should be revoked, which does often happen. Courts, however, have strong precedents to respect the right of biological parents in custody cases and other family legal matters. Therefore, stricter legal regulations for parenting are politically and practically infeasible. Would there be an undersecretary of parenting? Elected or appointed by whom? Whom would we trust to enforce such standards? Who would have the power to prevent people from having children if they did not parent by the book? The local police? A federal Parenting Patrol? Would people allow government intrusion into such a personal aspect of their lives? Obviously not. We'd rather classify parenting under the "life, liberty and pursuit of happiness" category, allowing individuals to decide for themselves. The flip side of that privilege is that people have to fend for themselves when it comes to parenting. We all parent as we were parented. We often control our children as we were controlled and suffer through the same rebellion from our teenagers as our parents suffered from us. Without an alternative or learned skills, we can become resentful enough to resort to abuse as a reaction to our intense anger.

Kimberly relates:

In my first year as a counselor at Child Guidance of Orange County, California, I was pregnant with our first child. In a session one day a mother of a 3-year-old was seated across the desk. This mother said that when her child screamed bad names at her, she became so angry at him she felt like "throwing him against the wall." I was shocked to hear that a woman, supposedly endowed with loving maternal instincts, could even have such thoughts! It wasn't until we had our first of six children that I realized that maternal as well as paternal instincts can wear thin on occasions, particularly with 2- and 3-year-olds.

Bruce teaches international negotiations at a university business school, using the joke: "What's the difference between a terrorist and a two-year-old? You can negotiate with the terrorist." We often laugh at that vivid memory of Kimberly's, realizing that we ourselves could have reacted with the same anger as this mother if we had not developed the skills to act sensibly instead of destructively.

Along with the regulation of parenting discussion, note that the U.S. system of government does have strict penalties for a parent who abuses a child. If not thrown in jail, such offenders can be court-ordered to attend parenting classes. Although some parents learn to change their behavior, just as often, required attendance at these classes becomes a forced exercise, yielding little in the way of results. Treatment becomes a power struggle with the judge, who is viewed by the parents as a surrogate autocratic parent. The parents rebel by reverting to their old styles in the privacy of their own homes.

Kimberly relates:

Over the years, I have worked with court-referred parents who have abused their children. If they feel justified that their children "deserved what they got," they often remain in a state of denial about their autocratic parenting styles and the damage done physically and emotionally to their children. One such parent was referred to an associate of mine for severely beating his son who had wet his pants. They explored ways of encouraging the son to use the toilet, but the father only paid lip service to trying democratic techniques. His refusal to change cost him his relationship with his son and his ability to live in his home. He hoped to win the power struggle, but in doing so, he lost everything that was once important to him.

Training should start long before a problem turns into an abusive situation. Hospitals teach childbirth techniques to assist parents in bringing children into the world, but not in raising a child once he or she becomes part of the family. The childbirth class serves a short-term need. The latter would fulfill a more important long-term need. Think what could happen if parenting skills were taught with Lamaze classes. In the long run, perhaps fewer tax dollars would be spent on protective service agencies for the children of physically abusive or emotionally neglectful parents. To their credit, some church and community leaders are starting even earlier in the family life cycle to offer or strongly suggest premarital counseling to set the stage for a healthy parenting atmosphere (see "Your Marriage Matters in Parenting").

In the next century, perhaps less money could be spent on alternative high schools, campus metal detectors, and security patrols if school curricula included parenting skills for students in the usual home economics courses. The value of cooking and sewing as skills pales in comparison to parenting. As a start, we've seen some schools instruct students to care for a fragile egg. The egg, in a container, is tied to the wrist of a student, who must carry it for a week without breaking it.

Democracy, Family Style

Ideally, in a family democracy, every person is treated with dignity and respect. No one person is inherently of greater or lesser worth than any other individual in the family. No parent should be considered more important than any child in the family, thereby receiving more respect than a child. Alternatively, no parent should lose respect from a child by becoming too permissive.

Mutual respect and example are keys to this. Parents cannot expect children to keep their rooms clean when their own room is a mess. Parents cannot demand that children knock at the parents' door when parents barge into children's rooms. Standards must be established and applied equally. All family members should be equal in terms of respect. Just as our society is becoming increasingly intolerant of racism and sexism, corresponding discriminatory attitudes (call it "childism") degrade our homes.

Kimberly relates:

A father enrolled in one of my parenting classes demanded that his children keep their rooms clean, but claimed it was his privilege to keep his own room filthy. This lack of basic understanding caused major conflict in his home, because the children thought it extremely unfair for the father to set rules for them that didn't apply to him. Rebellion, lack of respect, and even violence became common in the day-to-day life in that home. All three children had been in and out of in-patient psychiatric institutions from early ages. I introduced to both parents a less hypocritical approach. After learning and implementing what we are calling democratic parenting styles, this family made major strides toward mutual respect and family cooperation.

Representative Voice

A key principle in a democracy is representation of individual voice through collective bodies such as the U.S. Senate and House of Representatives. Regular meetings are held to formulate laws and revise them, resolve national problems, and discuss goals and future direction for our nation. These items are voted on and the rules stand until another act of Congress supersedes them. Although this system is fraught with its own problems, most Americans prefer it to a dictatorship. Businesses, schools, and other organizations hold regular staff meetings to coordinate their efforts. Without such coordination, these organizations can fall apart easily. Yet how often do families, the basic units of society, meet to organize themselves? Just like a well-run company or nation, families must also be organized along representative lines where every voice can be heard on a regular basis. Emotions can be vented appropriately, conflicts resolved, chores distributed fairly, and family fun planned.

Checks and Balances

Naturally, a system of checks and balances of the legislative, judicial, and executive branches are in place, which can be similarly implemented in the home. A rule suggested by children that is not in the best interest of the family can be vetoed by parents, such as "We want ice cream and cake for breakfast." In one family we know, the children chose a "no TV for one day" penalty for fighting with siblings. The rule didn't work for two reasons: It wasn't severe enough to stop the behavior, and the working parents were not around after school to enforce it. In the "Holding Family Meetings" chapter, we discuss how to democratically set rules and routines that all family members can live with.

Privileges and Penalties

All citizens in a democracy have privileges as well as responsibilities. Some individuals acquire higher levels of responsibilities and opportunities requisite to their maturing. For example, training for and receiving a driver's license is a big event in a youth's life—if he or she can demonstrate proficiency and knowledge of driving. Another is the privilege to vote at age 18. These opportunities are available to all members of society upon reaching the accountable age by law if they show themselves worthy of such privileges, particularly driving. Since driving is a privilege and not a right, many democratic parents require their teens to demonstrate responsibility in areas such as chores, homework completion, and room cleaning before the teens are able to add extra privileges—such as driving the family car—which are extended as long as they handle the privilege with responsibility.

Bruce relates:
I remember as a 16-year-old finally getting my hands on that invaluable piece of fresh new plastic—my driver's license—then, shortly after, letting the car run out of gas on the way home one day. My father, without ranting and raving, explained that letting the car get so low on gas when my

mother and sister might drive the car next was a bad thing. He asked me what punishment I thought would be fair, to which I suggested revoking my driving privileges for a long time, to which he agreed. I felt much worse imposing my own penalty than receiving one from him, especially since he was so calm. I have never—although I've sometimes come close—run out of gas again in my life.

The same principle applies to families as children show increased maturity—even very young children. Bedtimes can be extended when children take responsibility for getting up on time in the morning. Parents often increase allowances as children take on more household responsibilities, and in-family baby-sitting responsibilities can be shared and even paid for at an appropriate age.

On the other hand, we are all subject to the same consequences and penalties if we choose to violate a law once given these responsibilities. If we speed all the time, sooner or later, we will suffer the consequences—a ticket, a fine, and a rate increase or cancellation from our insurance company if the problem persists. Not only may the insurance company revoke their services, a judge may temporarily or permanently revoke our driver's license along with the privilege of driving. In a family democracy, special opportunities and responsibilities can also be revoked if abused or violated. For example, late curfews for teenagers may be revoked if they abuse the curfew hour. In our own family, we have a rule that if you can't be nice to your family, you can't enjoy the privilege of being nice to your friends. Our children have learned quickly that if they violate this rule, they must rescind their positive RSVPs to slumber parties and outings.

Kimberly relates:
Recently, I met with a court-referred couple. The husband was court restrained from seeing his wife and children because he was physically abusing his wife. The husband was enraged that this privilege had been temporarily revoked. I attempted to explain to him that someone needed

> *to protect his wife from abuse since he demonstrated that he*
> *could not. I further explained that by court order the privi-*
> *lege of being with his wife and children would not be rein-*
> *stated until he learned more appropriate ways to treat his*
> *family.*

Children should be taught that all family members are responsible for their own belongings and domain and share in responsibility for common areas. Responsible members of society are trained not to damage other people's property and are taught respect for community property such as parks, schools, and churches.

Financial Responsibility

Sometime during high school or upon completing college or professional education, people become gainfully employed as members of society's workforce. Society members are compensated financially according to their function, age, experience, and the quality and amount of their work. Citizens receive the benefit of being tax-paying members of society by using common roads, utilities, and other governmental services. Likewise, children, at the appropriate age, can be taught this financial order of society in the family model. Most experts agree that this is around age 4 or 5, but the only correct time is when children show an interest in the subject and are ready to enter a scaled-down version of the workforce.

One way of accomplishing this is through the traditional allowance that children receive for chores done around the house. An allowance should not be merely a dole, since getting something for nothing is not a value we want to see our children develop. Rather, payment should be given for completion of age-appropriate chores, which are checked for quality and consistency. If a job is not completed or is done sloppily, a sum should be deducted from that week's allowance or opportunities given to correct the situation. General guidelines for the amount deducted or second chances given should not be arbitrary, but agreed upon in advance. The same should apply to excessive, unnecessary reminders. The concept of our family job chart is discussed in the "Holding Family Meetings" chapter, but our kids know that a job is not done nor will it be paid for until the job is marked off the chart. A child receives no compensation for the week until the weekly Saturday jobs are done. If the child doesn't start the day's work at the agreed-upon time, allowing for an after-school snack first, she gets no snack time the next day. On the other hand, if every job is completed well, marked off, and no reminders or extra fines for misbehavior have been assessed, then the child gets a four-dollar bonus for the week, not a small sum for the younger children. The idea is to show children that as in the adult workplace, if they work hard and do their best, they will be rewarded. If they do not, they will face the consequences. Children who are supported by their well-meaning parents for years into their adulthood have not learned how the world works. As the old parable goes, gulls at some point stop catching fish for their young and start teaching them how to fish. You never stop being a parent, but at some point, you need to stop being the dole if your children are going to function in a dysfunctional world.

None of this is to suggest that the necessities of life for children such as shelter, food, and basic clothing should be reduced to terms of rent and overhead expense charged to each child. Children should feel that they are loved and are secure from an early age, not employees to help pay the family bills. Beyond basic needs, however, children can and need to be taught how to earn and save for extra purchases such as a special candy bar or a pair of "killer" earrings. Children can thus learn to discern the crucial difference between *needs* and *wants*, one of life's most important emotional skills. We all know children who become increasingly selfish by receiving everything they want. Some of these children actually get depressed if they don't have the right tennis shoes or jeans. These children can grow up to be adults with compulsive spending patterns and credit problems. Our own parents were financially conservative, asking us our plans for the summer for earning money. Bruce started a lawn care business and painted buildings—even picked pineapples in Hawaii one summer. Kimberly was a waitress and made and sold crafts. We worked hard to earn our own new ski equipment or extra clothes we *wanted* beyond the necessities.

Kids need to learn that even the necessities—food, clothing, and shelter—cost money. One Christmas morning years ago, despite warnings not to play near the house, our 7-year-old son carelessly sent his brand new regulation NHL hockey puck on its maiden voyage through the living room window. Since that accident was preventable if he had heeded the warnings, we had the repairman hand our son the bill. We then made a chart showing how much the window cost (about $70) and put him on a schedule to gradually earn the price of the window he broke.

Bruce relates:

As a former banker, when I talk about financial responsibility to the Boy Scouts or to other youth groups, I always tell them, "It's not how much you make that matters; it's how much you end up keeping." Teens need to be taught some of the basics such as balancing a checking account. They need to learn that filling out and returning every credit card application is like financial cocaine. "Just say no." I try to teach them about the "facts of life" of interest—letting it work for them brings the magic of compounding. Letting it work against them (24 hours a day without a day off) brings the suffocating pressure of debt. We've taught our kids by example that paying over 18 percent interest on credit card debt makes absolutely no sense. We've always paid our monthly balances in full, using credit cards only for convenience. When our teen daughter, seeing the neighbor's teen drive off in a new sports car, asked, "What car do I get when I'm 16?" I responded, "If you're responsible, you may use the family van, which is paid for and works just fine." We also believe having teens pay their own car insurance is a great idea. Our children know that good grades will keep their insurance rates down.

According to the *Houston Chronicle*, the average public university graduate in 1996 had $11,950 in debt and the private school student had $14,290. Not all of that comprised educational loans. Students get dozens of credit card offers in a given year. Nancy Deevers, director of education for the Consumer Credit Counseling Service of Northeastern Ohio, says, "It's almost like the 'I'll deal with it tomorrow' attitude runs the gamut from credit cards to student loans, and the maturity just isn't there. I wonder if it's a misery-loves-company thing, where everybody else is doing it, so it's no big deal." A 1996 survey by VISA showed that 8.7 percent of all people who filed for bankruptcy were under the age of 25.

As they watch parents and peers, young people can acquire an ear for the siren's song of consumer debt long before that first pre-approved credit card application arrives in the mail. Fifty-six percent of Americans carry a balance on their credit card of an average of $1,500, and almost 70 percent of people under age 35 do so, compared with only 18 percent of people over 75. Responsible children raised in a democratic home receive only what they need as they contribute to the family and earn what they want beyond that. They appreciate what they save for and purchase because they worked for it themselves—there is a sense of responsibility and productive pride.

Just as the opportunity exists in some employment situations for overtime work and time-and-a-half-pay, extra jobs may be provided to children for some discretionary income or to put toward major purchases such as a pet or a bicycle. These extra jobs, however, should be available only after regular responsibilities are completed. Dad generally shouldn't be throwing a garage sale for extra spending money until he has gone to work that week. Mom and Dad's income is used to pay true needs such as the mortgage and food. Extra money is for special wants such as that new set of golf clubs.

What is the work of children? In their preschool years, the answer is play. After entering school, however, their regular job is attending school and doing their homework. This should be completed before doing their chores for allowance, working at extra jobs for discretionary purchases, or playing with their friends for fun. If parents establish this pattern of priorities, children will see the natural order in their later lives. Children can't stay home from school to do extra jobs any more than Dad can stay home from work to hold a garage sale.

The connection between school and work can be strengthened as children become adolescents and the subject of college costs comes up. Credit from scholarships is no different than cash from savings when it comes to paying college tuition. Most universities require transcripts starting from the ninth grade in consideration for admissions and scholarships. Children who are capable, which includes most, can be taught to work with their heads instead of their backs and hands to earn scholarships to pay at least some of their college tuition and living expenses. We begin this training at a very young age. Paying kids for grades in the traditional sense, such as $10 for every A grade, is counterproductive because that diverts what should be intrinsic motivation and satisfaction for doing well in school. It turns life into a series of cash-for-good-behavior swaps, such as "How much money do I get if I stay off drugs?"—in an extreme sense. We do, however, award "scholarship" money for good grades—$10 for an A, but not in cash. Rather, our kids watch us write out the checks for their college savings accounts or their portions of extracurricular trips with the school science club or band.

In the increasingly competitive arena of higher education, many might complain that scholarships are out of their reach. However, this is simply not true. Many internet-based search services and other resources list scholarship funds (even small ones) that often go begging for a recipient year after year.

If, on the other hand, children choose to spend their high school years partying their brains out instead of applying those brains to their studies, they need to experience the consequence of earning their share with part-time employment in college. Alternatively, the child should be required to take out student loans for which he or she is responsible for paying off in the years following college—ten years in most cases. Most children will quickly decide these alternatives are less preferable. This is not to suggest that adolescents keep their noses in the books every weekend. A healthy amount of extracurricular activities is as critical to the high school experience as classes are. Many college admission boards look for these activities that indicate a balanced student.

There are other benefits of having children provide at least some of their college tuition either by scholarship, part-time work, or student debt. Children will most likely appreciate and take full advantage of their college education if their sacrifice is more than just time spent. Statistics show that students are taking more years, on average, to get through college, perhaps an indication of a lack of direction, concern for accumulated debt, or concern about education. For all these reasons, Kimberly finished her undergraduate degree at BYU in three years knowing that years of graduate school and expense lay ahead. Children who can truly appreciate college when surrounded by apathetic students will not only have an enriching college experience, but will also apply themselves to their careers and personal lives in future years.

Times of External Crisis

In our nation's past, economic troubles, wars, and epidemics have created crisis and confusion. At these difficult times, the federal government enacts legislation believed to be in the best interest of our country. These bills are then signed by the president. We remember the days of the 1970s oil shocks when Congress reduced the highway speed limit to 55 miles an hour. One year during that era, President Jimmy Carter asked the nation to scale back or forego outdoor Christmas lights in an effort to conserve energy. The Great Depression was another, more severe crisis. These were typically days of great sacrifice for the American people as they pulled together for the common good.

Times of external crisis come for families, too, mostly beyond the control of family members. These crises include financial hardship due to unemployment, sickness, or career changes. Like the country, the family may be asked to make sacrifices to move through difficult times to better days. At such times, however, presidential

leadership is often called for. The nature and degree of these sacrifices, along with a plan for recovery, should not be dictated by power
figures in the parent ruling body. Franklin Roosevelt provided the
leadership and inspiration for the various public policy initiatives,
but Congress, the people's representatives, passed the legislation, as is
the case with any law. Likewise, a plan in the family for dealing with
a crisis should be enacted through a democratic process. The setting
of a family meeting or special family council devoted exclusively to
this purpose would be the best channel to resolve the crisis. The
weekly family meeting should be a regular activity, not held only in
times of crisis.

This special crisis meeting should begin with a candid discussion of the problem at hand. The degree to which the problem is
divulged depends on the nature of the problem and the maturity of
the children involved. Most families in crisis, however, find that children can handle a higher degree of problem detail than the parents
might expect. Parents might worry, "If I tell the children too much, it
could upset them." In extreme cases, this could be true, but more
often, an opposite problem occurs. That is, parents do not disclose
enough information, which the children can sense. This makes children more anxious and upset than knowing more of the details,
calmly and fully explained to them by parents.

One of Kimberly's clients was the husband and father in a family of four, for whom life was not extraordinary until his elderly parents experienced severe health difficulties. The grandfather had a
stroke, and the grandmother, while taking care of her husband, fell
and broke her hip. The son, his wife, and two children met and decided to pitch in with the necessary help until the crisis was over. The
whole family, including the children, took turns doing laundry,
cleaning house, cooking and serving meals, and so forth. The grandfather eventually recovered from the stroke to a great extent, and the
grandmother's hip healed. Ties in and among all three generations
were strengthened by pulling together as an entire family in that time
of health crisis.

In our own family, the birth of twins in 1993, besides being twice the fun, brought on extra challenges and stress in the home, much more so than with a single birth. The time and effort necessary to get things done was squared, not doubled. A 30-minute preparation for church or other outing now took 90 minutes. Each night we had to decide which parent would sacrifice sleep. One night Bruce picked up the wrong baby for feeding. That twin was sleeping instead of crying, but not for long—soon both babies were wailing! We nicknamed diapers "jet fuel," because first, we went through them at an alarming rate; second, and more important, if we ran out, the household crash and burn was ugly! We laugh about that period now, but those months were times of serious physical and emotional challenge for our family.

We tried to involve the other children in the solution to the excess demands brought on by the blessing of twins in the house. In preparing for our third child's fourth birthday party, it was obvious we would need help cleaning the house and making other preparations. We explained our feelings and the situation to our two older children, ages six and nine. They sailed into the work with a great spirit of cooperation and cleaned the entire house for the party themselves. Other examples in our home abounded during this so-called period of crisis, until the twins got a little older.

Children are masters at picking up nonverbal or voice-activated cues from their parents. Since a high percentage of communication is non-verbal, such as tone of voice or posture, they know if there is more to the story. Try to avoid their assuming the worst—"If Dad loses his job, do we have to live on the street?"—by telling your kids directly what will actually happen. Parents must learn to couch explanations in terms of "might" or "could" or "probably" happen when addressing the most likely outcomes. The lines of communication should be kept open, and fears should be addressed to avoid compounding them. Questions should be dealt with immediately and frankly, with the appropriate amount of genuine reassurance that in the long run, the family will survive the crisis.

Life is ambiguous, and teaching children early to deal with an uncertain future will serve them well as adults. Allowing children to responsibly face crises in the family teaches them to handle their own difficulties later in life. They will be more likely to successfully handle life's vagaries without panic, calmly plotting their course to resolve whatever steps are necessary. Surely in the twenty-first century, careers and other life choices will become more, not less, ambiguous, which makes teaching children valuable coping skills even more important.

After the extent of a crisis is candidly explained to the children, parents should next explore the options available to the family, if indeed there are more than one. The next course of action may be so logical or obvious that discussion of alternatives would be counterproductive. For example, transferring within a company might be a logical alternative to unemployment. However, other viable alternatives, such as looking for new employment or Mother temporarily going back to work until Dad retrains for another job, should be discussed as a family, with guidance from the parents. Family discussion makes children feel a part of the solution, not merely victims of circumstance. If there is only one truly viable alternative, the reasons for taking a course of action, and for not taking another, should be carefully explained.

The discussion should then focus on possible ways for all family members to contribute to the solution. If everyone needs to tighten the belt, for example, parents will likely be impressed by children's creative ideas to help, ranging from paper routes to recycling. During the setback, the sacrifices children are willing to make, such as extra chores for less allowance, can be touching, drawing family members closer through thick and thin as crises come and go. Contrast this with the destructive effect financial or health-related crises can have as they pull apart families that have not learned to pull together.

If managed wisely, hard times of various kinds can have a unifying and an uplifting influence on the family unit as a whole. This is comparable to the euphoria an entire nation feels after coming through a crisis such as war or depression with a renewed sense of hope for the future.

Consistency and Gambling

Autocratic governments control and force compliance. Often the punishment is arbitrary, unfair, and implemented through tyrannical coercion. A true democracy permits choice within the constraints of mutually agreed upon laws enacted for the common good. Democracy breaks down if the enforcement of consequences and application of penalties are missing or at best inconsistent. We all see speed limit signs yet often choose to break the law if we think there is a low probability of getting caught, such as speeding in a remote area. During the Los Angeles riots of 1992, Bruce was working in downtown Los Angeles and remembers seeing burned out police cars and piles of shattered glass from rampages. Hoodlums and looters engaged in criminal activity, not realizing that in many cases they were caught on tape. Likewise, if we think there is low probability of a harsh penalty, we are less inclined to fear the consequences of the law. While it is true that judges operate within a certain range of sentencing, depending on the circumstances of the crime, the penalty is carefully spelled out and far from arbitrary.

The odds of winning the grand prize in most state lotteries approach infinitesimal odds, millions to one. The probability of being struck by lightning in a lifetime is only 600,000 to 1. Yet people continue to buy lottery tickets, hoping they might "get away" with millions. If children think the odds of getting away with misbehavior are substantially better, say 1 in 2 or 3, it is no surprise that children continue to "play the lottery" by misbehaving again and again.

If a family democracy is to be successful, consequences must be applied consistently and fairly each time a family member chooses to break a law or rule established at a family meeting. In the hectic days of rearing children, parents can become lax and inconsistent in their application of consequences, typically because it would require too much time and effort to enforce the rules. These same parents eventually find themselves dealing with even more frustration than the effort spent initially. We can't stress this point enough, because children will repeat the same misbehavior if they think the consequence will not be applied. They will also be less likely to heed reminders or warnings about the impending consequence if they don't conform.

In a family democracy, laws must be spelled out and cannot be arbitrary or vague. One problem in our democracy is that some laws can be ambiguous and left up to much interpretation and manipulation by politicians and lawyers (that's why we have so many). Laws established in family meetings, discussed in the chapter "Holding Family Meetings," must be clear, concise, and consistently applied so that family order is maintained.

Liberty's Light in the Family

Despite severe transition pains, the fall of communism in the former USSR showed the world that centrally, tightly controlled economies and ideologies do not work. As a college student, Bruce visited Moscow and Leningrad during the height of the cold war. Everyone had a job, including the woman selling ice cream on the corner in December, but people were dissatisfied, as the events later in the 1980s testified. Democracy has become the model for most of the world's nations, and those countries without it witness waves of emigration to democratic nations. There is a reason for this. People the world over covet the representative voice, mutual respect, privilege to vote, and the consistency in the application of the laws that Americans enjoy.

Likewise, in our families, we should make our homes havens of democratic rule, not autocratic tyranny, to avoid the problems non-democratic families face. Children cannot typically migrate from homes until of legal age, but they can flee emotionally at almost any stage of life. The effort that most parents expend to keep their children in line could all go to naught if the children flee psychological borders to seek refuge elsewhere, such as in peer groups or through substance abuse. Until that 2 percent number of democratically run families truly grows, the number of emotional refugees will continue to increase. Teenagers will continue to run away, and the teen pregnancy rate will continue to rise as youth seek in vain the comfort of someone to love and respect them.

In Kimberly's therapy practice over the years, she has attempted to pick up the pieces of families in which parents have haphazardly approached their responsibility of child raising or have left their responsibility to others. This book provides skills and tools for parents to help their families function more peacefully. Our cities can only become more peaceful as parents become trained in the most important responsibility that transcends the generations. True democracy with liberty and justice for all must begin within the walls of our own homes, regardless of the dysfunctional chaos outside them.

Two

Why Children Misbehave

Nature versus Nurture

To explain children's behavior, conventional wisdom uses reasons often ranging from simplistic to ridiculous. Many explanations come down to a nature-versus-nurture argument. On the one hand, proponents of the nature theory propose that heredity and preprogrammed characteristics play the dominant role in determining one's behavior. "He was born that way" explains a person's actions. According to this theory, children are like snowflakes, each coming to earth with distinct differences, which are apparent from the hospital nursery on.

On the other hand, the nurture side of the story argues that environment determines a child's personality. Individual characteristics develop directly from the events and situations one experiences. Rather than snowflakes, children are more like lumps of clay that can be molded and formed into personalities as unique as the set of circumstances from which a person emerges. This theory, however, raises a puzzling question: Why do individuals react with wide variations to similar environmental circumstances?

The debate is important, but endless. Most people acknowledge that behavior is a genuine mix of the two elements, but also admit the impossibility of determining the precise percentage each element contributes. Similarly, after taking a taste of pudding, it's impossible to say just how many eggs and exactly how much milk is in the food.

That the pudding does contain eggs and milk could be detected, but that's as far as hindsight taste could go without the recipe. In addition, those who believe that behavior is merely "caused" exclusively, by either internal or external forces, fail to see the creative capabilities of individuals to make decisions—to choose how they will respond to innate or environmental conditions—changing the "mix" on their own, so to speak.

The debate is more interesting when applied to children because they have had less experience to account for their behavior. In adults, we find it easier to attribute behavior to long-established patterns and years of experience. With children, however, we all know of infants raised in similar environments, in the same homes, for example, with widely varying personality traits. Studies of identical twins, who have the same genetic makeup, debate the mix of nature versus nurture in personality development.

In our own family, our twins, now age 5, although not identical nor even the same gender, provide an interesting case study in the debate. One is outgoing, the other more reserved; one adventuresome, the other hesitant to explore. They have been raised in the same family, have had the same physical environment, and have had the same school and church teachers so far, and yet they display incredibly different personalities. As toddlers, she threw kisses; he threw toys. She eats the salad; he eats the croutons. During the Halloween door-to-door ritual last year, she made the introductions; he exchanged treats he didn't like for better ones at each new house—trick or trade!

Some would argue that we treat the twins differently, which may be true. Although experts generally recognize that children are born with certain traits of temperament, direct inheritance of personality traits has never been established. If behavior is primarily the result of heredity, why can children of the same family, like ours, have such different personalities? The "recipe" for children simply does not exist.

Stages

Parents also hear much about ages and stages, such as the Terrible Twos. An anxious parent may receive advice, such as "Don't worry—

she's just going through a stage," or "All boys his age do that—he'll grow out of it." Experience exposes the sad reality and false hope of many parents in that the child never does grow out of it. Instead, the child is more likely establishing a pattern of behavior for life. Although children do appear to have slightly differentiated stages of oppositional reaction to adults, age should not be used as a reason for accepting inappropriate behavior. Often it is not just a normal stage to be expected and excused. Many parents blame childhood stages rather than their own permissive parenting. They hope their children will grow out of the stage, but they find that the behavior only worsens with time.

Kimberly relates:

I worked with a family whose 4-year-old son had been physically aggressive with his sibling at home when he didn't get his way. This behavior had now begun manifesting itself in his preschool program and was worsening by the day. His parents had always heard that boys are more aggressive than girls, and they hoped that this behavior was a stage their son was going through. After he had thrown a chair across the room during a time-out in the principal's office, they called their pediatrician, who referred them to me. Limits were appropriately established, consequences were implemented, and only then did his behavior improve. He was a much happier child, because other children had been scared of his aggressiveness and stayed away. He was sporting a bully label that would have stayed with him for a long time.

Behaviors continue in people as long as that behavior serves its purpose. Not only children but also adults are known to occasionally use temper tantrums and whining to win arguments with their spouses or others. We know a wife who once threw drinking glasses at her husband to get his attention. As long as the behavior achieves its goal, people of all ages will continue to use it. The key is finding the motivation behind the behavior.

We need to realize that our children's misbehavior is not the result of an age or a stage. It may be typical and recurrent but should not be accepted nor considered normal. Parents who understand the goals of children's behavior and misbehavior are often able to influence their children in positive directions.

Teachers can also be helpful in spotting negative behaviors and alerting parents to help end the pattern of behavior as soon as possible. Kimberly has worked with several gifted teachers who are able to spot a child's goal behind the misbehavior. One of these teachers, actually one of our son's fourth-grade teachers, would require the misbehaving child seeking the class's attention to immediately stop the behavior and write down what she had been doing and why it was wrong. This gives immediate feedback to the child about the behavior and teaches her to be less impulsive. During a missed recess, the child has time to think about what happens if he or she commits second or third offenses. We not only allow but encourage the teachers of our children to enforce this type of strictness on a child for not completing assigned work or other school misbehavior. We find that the teachers welcome this support from home.

Immediate feedback about your child's behavior from teachers helps identify the goal your child is trying to achieve by misbehaving. We have been very blessed in having teachers for our children who are willing to give timely feedback to us as parents. We feel it's important to deal with behavioral problems in a team effort with all caregivers concerned. Our combined efforts stop the problem much quicker—not allowing it to become a habit or personality trait. In our home, consequences for misbehavior always have an essay component to them.

The essay written by our children includes:
1. A few sentences listing exactly what they did wrong, whose rights were violated, and in what way
2. Why it was wrong
3. What they should do differently in the future

Younger children who are not yet able to write can verbalize their responses to these questions to a parent. This exercise also allows children to bring their behavior to a conscious level. If the essay is not sincerely written, they get a chance to try again. If a younger child responding to the questions is not sincere, he or she must take time-out until the parent is ready for the child to come back and try the exercise again. If parents consistently follow through, children learn to do it right the first time. If the behavior is discovered and dealt with as soon as it begins, this accountability measure helps end the behavior, or so-called stage.

Goal Motivation

Instead of the age-old, inconclusive, impossible debate on nature versus nurture, human behavior can be better explained in terms of its pattern and the personal purpose it serves. For example, to understand a child's current behavior, parents should not seek answers simply from past behavior—"He's always been a hothead." Instead, parents should look for the underlying purpose of the behavior that serves the child. The behavior is not random nor is it meaningless. It indicates and achieves an end for the child. It brings about a certain benefit. When parents are able to pinpoint the child's goal inherent in the behavior, they gain insight into reasons for the child's behavior.

To illustrate, some parents and counselors look for causes of low academic achievement in a child whose high IQ test scores indicate a high level of ability. Rather than looking for causes, we would suggest looking for goals that the behavior achieves. That is, how does the behavior (in this instance, low achievement) specifically serve the child who exhibits it?

Surprisingly, it might make complete sense from the child's perspective to underachieve for one of several reasons.

1. The child could gain control and power over those people, such as teachers or parents, who want the child to do better.
2. The child could receive special attention from those same teachers and parents.

3.   Underachievement may serve to excuse the child from functioning at capacity, providing an escape from rigorous academic exercises for gifted children. Understanding this goal helps stop labels like "stupid" or "slow learner" when the child could be anxious about his abilities or even manipulative.

4.   Intentionally low scores may be used to get even with the parents who, from the child's viewpoint, have coerced academic achievement upon the child. Low achievement is often a bright child's weapon of choice, since the parents are typically educated themselves and value education highly. This type of behavior pains parents most. Therefore, the child elects to use it to serve his purpose.

Training is the key to recognize and understand the goals behind a child's misbehavior, which helps parents direct future behavior.

The Four Goals of Misbehavior

Many child psychologists agree that the goals of children who misbehave can be classified into four groups: attention, power, revenge, and support. The key to understanding the goal behind your child's misbehavior is to recognize your feelings at that time.

- If you feel *annoyed* or *irritated* at your child's requests, the goal is probably to receive *attention.*
- If you feel *anger* and a desire to win back *control,* the goal is likely *power.*
- If you feel *hurt* and *outraged* by your child's behavior, the goal is most likely *revenge.*
- If you feel *discouraged* and *helpless* when confronted by your child's apparent inabilities, the child's goal is probably to *dodge responsibility* or *seek support.*

Let's look at these four goals in detail:

1. *Attention—needing to be noticed and served.* In the drive for attention, the child gains the notice of others by clowning, misbehav-

ing, or disturbing in some way. You can recognize your child's attempts for attention in nonproductive behavior when you become increasingly annoyed, irritated, and impatient. By attempting to stop the misbehavior, the child gets the attention she wants. The behavior stops temporarily, but resurfaces later, sometimes in a different form, when the child feels a renewed need for attention.

Examples:
- In trying to put a child to bed, a mother reads the child a story and hears, "Just one more story, Mommy, please!" After that issue has been settled, the child may then say, "I need a drink now." After getting the child a drink, a few minutes later the mother may hear, "Can I go to the bathroom?" The child probably has neither a dry throat nor a full bladder, but wants attention and uses these methods to get attention.
- A 14-year-old boy in therapy continually forgot his math book because he enjoyed hearing his teacher's daily announcement to the entire class: "And guess who forgot his math book again!" The boy's behavior in this and other forms increased because he enjoyed the attention he was getting from these performances. He even commented that someday he would like to be an actor.
- For eighteen months after the birth of her younger brother, a 3-year-old girl continually picked at scabs on her face, causing fresh bleeding. Her attentive parents thought this was a sign of a definite psychological disorder, because they could not stop the behavior with any combination of rewards or punishment. After talking with the child, it was suggested that this was an attention-getting behavior, which the parents were advised to simply ignore. When they did, the behavior stopped.

Kimberly relates:
One of my clients, a 10-year-old boy, suddenly became unable to go to bed at night without a parent in the room. He would awaken his parents often after midnight when they were asleep in their own beds, claiming he was scared

and asking them to go to the bathroom with him. Though these behaviors appeared to be manipulating, this child was unaware that his fears were unconscious efforts to get the parents to spend extra time with him, making them attentive and available. In our first therapy session together, he was able to identify his goal of getting attention and to find the solution: time with mom and dad. His loving but busy parents realized that spending time with their son after school instead of after midnight was just what he and they needed. Once a routine of regular and generous amounts of time was established, his night terrors ended.

The attention-getting goal is becoming more prevalent with more parents both working outside the home. We address this subject in depth later in this chapter. Children find many creative ways to get the attention of their parents, very often through negative means. If you make time that is consistent, children will make fewer negative bids for attention. It takes organization and planning on the part of parents, but it's worth it. The most important scheduling parents can do is to allow time with their children. It cuts down on attention-getting behaviors.

A child should not receive attention when making a negative bid for it. Nagging, reminding, reprimands, and punishment are all forms of attention children actively or subconsciously seek. Often, there is no apparent reason that the child would feel a need for more attention. However, a new baby, a divorce, or trips by parents alone can each increase a child's need for attention. Understanding the child's goal of attention can help diagnose the problem quickly.

Bruce relates:

When I was a graduate student, we took our infant son to the health center for an infected toenail. The problem recurred a few times, giving him some extra attention he apparently grew to enjoy. Occasionally, as an older child, he would try to invoke the "toe-owie" reason for wanting to

> *stay up or get our attention. When we realized that his goal was parental attention and not medical attention, the behavior stopped when we ignored him. Instead, we gave him attention at other times when he wasn't making an inappropriate bid for it.*

Before inappropriate behaviors become habitual, parents must act immediately, by ignoring misbehaviors not imminently dangerous or by issuing consequences for continuing behaviors, such as assigning an essay as discussed previously.

Another way of curbing misbehavior is by giving positive attention before the child behaves in negative ways, as in the example of the 10-year-old boy discussed previously. This breaks the connection between behavior and attention and stops the child's expectation of receiving attention on demand. Most important, parents should not react by rewarding negative behaviors with any form of attention. This is exactly what the child wants and he will continue the misbehavior until the pattern is changed.

2. *Power—attempting to control as the child has felt controlled.* A child can be openly disobedient and stubborn, showing what is called passive resistance by not doing what he or she is asked. He or she may continue to misbehave or may stop temporarily, only to later intensify the behavior in order to win. You can recognize the goal of power when you as the parent feel angry and resentful. You may feel a desire to establish or regain control.

Examples:
- A child who desires a toy while shopping with his mother at the market keeps insisting on the toy and throws a temper tantrum when his mother says no. As the tantrum continues, his mother buys the toy to avoid further public embarrassment. The child has achieved control of the situation by getting the desired toy by throwing the tantrum.
- A teenager actively ignores an early parental curfew and then

pretends to have forgotten the agreed-upon time. Through not keeping the curfew by passively forgetting, the child controls the schedule and comes home when he pleases.

To understand the goal of power and to prevent further damage to family relationships, parents need to realize that the issue is not solved by either fighting or giving in. Coercion may bring about a form of cooperation, but internal cooperation and true harmony in the home will not be achieved. Autocratic parents win the war but lose the relationship. Dictatorial edicts in emotional displays of anger only increase the children's drive for power and do nothing but escalate the conflict. On the other hand, overly permissive parents lose the respect of their children and themselves. They are merely compliant innkeepers, with the children easily achieving the goal of control.

The concept of winning and losing must be eliminated to develop successful family relationships. Parents need to withdraw from power struggles and concentrate on turning a potentially violent situation into a stronger family relationship. Autocratic commands only create a higher level of power struggle and decrease children's self-esteem as a member of the family. If children continue to lose these power struggles, they may change their goal of power to the more destructive goal of revenge if they feel unloved.

3. *Revenge—hurting self or others through disobedience or delinquent behavior.* In extreme cases, a child with this goal may become violent or severely depressed as a way of expressing defiance. The goal is to strike back and get even with perceived injustices done to them. In response, you as a parent may feel hurt and enraged. If a parent attempts to get even, the child often seeks further revenge by using the same or a different weapon. This is because the child's belief that he is unloved has been reinforced by the parent's counterrevenge or angry behavior. By controlling their urge to retaliate, parents must stop this often violent, destructive cycle of behavior, a victim of which is naturally a child's self-esteem.

Examples:

- The daughter of a principal consciously makes no effort to pass the eighth grade by rebelling against her mother's attempts to force her to study diligently and to achieve at school.
- A toddler bites Mommy when she returns from work late. Not realizing his loneliness, the mother, reflecting the child's mood, screams at the child and slaps him. The child kicks her and later refuses to return her kiss at bedtime.
- The son of a policeman gets arrested for shoplifting to embarrass his father after the parent attempts to control with whom the son associates at school.

Children who resort to revenge are often cruel and disliked by others. When parents do not see or acknowledge the child's pain or retaliate against the child out of their own pain, the child often seeks further revenge by increasing the delinquent behavior or choosing another weapon.

Kimberly relates:

I once had a girl aged 16 in therapy who had been referred by her physician in the hope that emotional treatment might cure her symptoms of anorexia. The girl had a very controlling and rejecting father. He supervised her meals, chose her friends, and mistrusted her because she was headstrong and different from other children. During our first meeting, I diagnosed her as anorexic (refusing to eat). Unlike the other areas in her life, eating was something she felt she could control. Anorexia was brought on by her goal of revenge for her father's control over her life. Her father's failure to recognize this problem had produced the opposite effect he intended—she ate less and less until she was in serious physical jeopardy. In the next few months, her doctor put her on a rigid program of food intake to save her life. With her father's behavior unchanged and unable to use the

*old weapon of diet, the daughter chose a new weapon: preg-
nancy. When I talked with her about the consequences of
that action, she stated, "I don't care—I just want to get back
at him."*

Another example of revenge is the child who runs away. Some
children run away for attention, but most do so because they feel
unloved and therefore seek out someone who will love them. The
father of a 16-year-old girl we know said of his runaway daughter that
he knew where she was but had no intention of retrieving her. "She
can rot there—I'm not going to get her." The daughter had left home
because her father punished her for a C grade in school by taking
away for six months the horse she earned and loved. The father had
ignored the significance of the daughter's horse, which was her pre-
dominate love object. To solve the problem, the father could have
retrieved her from her hideout—she would return if asked—and
expressed his love. However, he refused and the relationship deterio-
rated from that point on, with the daughter using the more extreme
forms of revenge: drug and alcohol abuse.

4. Dodging responsibility or seeking support. Through their
behavior, such as acting like a baby, children who feel inadequate try
to convince others to expect nothing from them. Though these children's initial goal might be manipulation of parents and others, they
are often extremely discouraged and can ultimately give up all hope
of succeeding. Because others often do for them, these children often
feel they cannot accomplish tasks without the help of others.

Disappointments are part of life, but children who feel inadequate think that they have experienced more than their fair share.
Children can learn that life's disappointments aren't necessarily
aimed at them if parents acknowledge their children's discouragement and convince them that they are lovable and capable. Parents
must refrain from labeling and punishing a discouraged child, who
may give up entirely, feeling even more incapable and hopeless.
Parents should encourage all improvements, no matter how small.

Examples:

- Although a child is capable, he will not try new or challenging tasks. He has low self-esteem and believes his parents don't think he can perform the task. He continues to passively carry out normal but unchallenging tasks at school and at home.

- A child exhibits illness symptoms to stay home from school. As parents seek medical cures and keep the child from attending classes, the child begins to think she really is ill and develops a school phobia from the parents' anxiety, pity, and overprotection. The child never graduates from high school.

- Often children with special needs are handicapped not so much by their physical condition, but by their parents' pity. Not every handicapped child can be another Helen Keller, nor is every teacher Anne Sullivan. But placing low expectations on these special children can be very damaging. In general, handicapped children will rise to meet the realistic expectations of others. Parents should never label children or cause them to lose faith in themselves.

In short, to combat the goal of maintaining inadequacy, never do anything for a child that he can do for himself. Many parents mistakenly assume that a child will grow into a task or learn to do it later. The longer parents do things for children they can do for themselves, the more difficult it becomes for children to change this interpretation of life and learn to fit into a functioning society. These patterns of behavior can and do become habits and ultimately handicap children, who later become handicapped adults if the problem goes unresolved.

We know a girl who was an average student, the second-born in the family. Her older sibling was an excellent student. Janet was labeled by both parents and teachers as slow, and her classwork reflected her lack of belief in herself. When her parents were approached by the school to place the girl in remedial classes, they agreed, thinking they were doing the best thing for their daughter's future. This negative label remained until Janet was tested for high school class placement and was found to have a very high IQ.

Often parents don't know what to do with severely discouraged children. Although the parents may overtly state their belief in their child, if not sincere, the unspoken message from nonbelieving parents can actually reinforce the low self-image of the child. The best treatment for a child at this point is for parents to eliminate all criticism and to encourage any positive attempts. Parents need to focus on the efforts of the child, not necessarily the end result.

Another of Kimberly's therapy clients was a successful surgeon who placed second in a nationwide academic contest when she was in high school. After that performance, her parents matter-of-factly wanted to know how he could improve in next year's competition, since he had made *only* second place. This experience and other similar ones created self-doubt in this student and ultimately contributed to her lowered self-esteem as an adult. Parents with overly high expectations can cause the opposite effect on a discouraged child, who will lower his performance, thus lowering expectations. In school settings, such a child can be labeled a slow learner, which is actually untrue but reinforces beliefs of inadequacy.

To summarize, the following table should help you recognize which of the above four goals your child is pursuing.

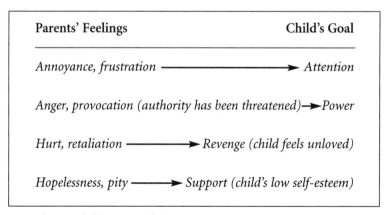

Parents' Feelings	Child's Goal
Annoyance, frustration	*Attention*
Anger, provocation (authority has been threatened)	*Power*
Hurt, retaliation	*Revenge (child feels unloved)*
Hopelessness, pity	*Support (child's low self-esteem)*

Thus, a child may misbehave to get attention, power, or revenge, not necessarily aimed at his parent but society at large. The misbehavior could also be a show of the child's lack of belief in himself, as if to say, "It's not my fault; I can't stop it."

Perceived Discouragement

The underlying cause of all four of the goals of misbehavior is the child's perceived discouragement. Any negative emotion can be dealt with in either a productive or contentious manner. The child will use and reuse whatever type of behavior works to achieve her goal—positive or negative in nature. Children are not instinctively bad, although like any natural organism, they are inclined to choose the path of least resistance. Typically, if a child is adequately encouraged, has a good work ethic, and believes in her own ability, the child is usually cooperative and works toward the common good of the family and society. On the other hand, a discouraged child refuses to cooperate. Often he has tried, but to no avail, to belong to the family and society by behaving in useful ways. If these useful and productive behaviors are not rewarded or noticed, the opposite occurs. This only perpetuates the refusal to cooperate.

For example, the dethroned first child may whine or regress in potty training. This is the eldest child's way of expressing discouragement for not getting the attention he was used to receiving. Other alternatives exhausted, the child resorts to seeking attention but in a negative way. Unknowing parents reinforce these behaviors by not dealing with the temporary discouragement directly. An attached label further discourages the child and creates an artificial stage, which the parent hopes in vain that the child will outgrow. Sadly, the child will continue in this stage of behavior because it becomes habitual. The longer the child acts in this manner, the harder it becomes to stop the negative habit or pattern.

When children adamantly defy parents, attempt to hurt themselves through self-mutilation or even suicide, harm others, or maintain poor grades despite high intellect, they often have been discouraged or overindulged. When parents attempt to force children to stop these negative behaviors, the effort can often backfire by increasing rebellion. The children often feel unloved and attempt to turn the control back to the parents by intensifying their behavior and by exerting their power.

This reaction of children can be at a conscious level, or more likely, at a subconscious level. For example, one of the teenage control pathologies of our day is eating disorders. Like other behaviors, eating can be controlled, which may subconsciously be used to hurt domineering authority figures.

Causes of Discouragement

Not enough attention. Perhaps from economic necessity, our nation is increasingly becoming a nation of two-career households. Many children are raised by "live-ins" or day care centers. Children spend increasingly precious little time with the most significant people in their lives—their parents. As a result, children may make bids for negative attention, believing this is the only way to get *any* attention. They become discouraged in their competition with other demands on their parents' time. As a result, these children may resort to hypochondria, whining, power struggles, and poor school performance to negatively involve the parent.

Too much money, not enough time. Paradoxically, trying to make up for a lack of time with children by giving them the material goods they want can have the opposite of the intended effect. It is indeed possible to spoil a child. Human want is infinite and can be instilled at a young age. Overindulged children become discouraged even though they have many possessions but lack something seen in the toy store, on TV, or in the homes of other children. They feel unhappy unless they have everything they want. These children have not distinguished between needs and wants—they perceive their wants as needs. Unavailable parents can mistakenly indulge children to ease the guilt that accompanies their unavailability. Children then misbehave to get what they perceive as basic needs but really are not.

Not enough control. Studies have shown that, surprisingly, children can become discouraged by too much permissiveness at home, because they assume that parents don't care enough about them to lay down commonsense ground rules. Studies also show that problem children who rebel would not have objected to obeying family rules in the home. Rules bring a sense of security and a feeling of parental concern. Children who don't have rules are more discouraged, more impulsive, and less well behaved than those children who must obey curfews or respect the property of other family members. The lack of rules, consistently applied, becomes a self-fulfilling prophecy that finds children disobeying simply because there were no rules to prevent the misbehavior. Children without limits and rules are today called permissively raised, and a large majority develop problems. Children who misbehave through lack of limits feel inadequate and unable to function in positive ways.

Too much autocratic control. Autocratic control discourages children by causing them to question their parents' love. An autocratically inconsistent style confuses children as to what is really expected of them. One day a parent might ignore misbehavior—the next day the child is severely punished for the same violation. It's like ticketing a jaywalker after letting him go the day before. By controlling children, they lack creativity, critical thinking, and decision-making skills. The key is finding the right balance between attention and control, which will lead to cooperation, not discouragement and misbehavior.

Discouragement and Divorce

Every year in the United States, the parents of over 1 million children divorce. The resulting emotional and behavioral problems among these children have become a serious concern. Over the past fifteen years, Kimberly has worked with hundreds of children of divorced families. Frustrated by the lack of control of an important relationship in their lives, these children sometimes suffer the most severe form of discouragement, which often necessitates therapy for working through the problem. Over the years, Kimberly has led many groups of children in confronting their parents' divorce and in working out the issues they face. These children are helped by universalizing their problems with other children dealing with the same issues. Many schools now offer similar programs to the growing number of children of divorced parents.

When parents divorce, children can feel torn between the two parents, feeling they must please both parents. When children can't simultaneously agree with each parent, they often feel guilty and even blame themselves for the divorce by reverting to thumb sucking, bed-wetting, or soiling their underwear. They may have sleeping difficulties or temper tantrums. They may fight, lie, steal, start fires, skip school, use drugs or cry excessively. They may also withdraw from friends or family. They can do poorly in school, become uncooperative, and retaliate by projecting their anger at their parents or themselves.

The symptoms children exhibit when their parents separate and divorce are so pervasive that children are often misdiagnosed with attention deficit disorder (ADD) and other disorders because of misbehavior due to their discouragement. Surprisingly, sometimes children of divorce do not misbehave at all, but instead, become extremely well behaved. They may be suppressing guilt for their parents' breakup. By being a model child, they hope to repair the damage and reverse the situation.

In confronting family crises, parents in a divorce situation should be as candid and honest as possible with their children. Without excessive dramatization or blame, the parents should explain to the child the reasons for the divorce. They could calmly set forth any details that might clarify and also ease the separation for their child.

The child must understand that the divorce had nothing to do with the parents' love for the child or with his behavior. Further, neither parent will ever stop loving the child, who is literally a part of each parent (emotionally, spiritually, and physically). To illustrate this for children in therapy, Kimberly will often hold three candles, representing two parents and their child. As each parent holds a lit candle, they combine their flames and then light the child's candle. This represents the love that brought the child into the world. The parents then blow out their candles, representing their love going away, while the child's candle remains lit.

Tempting as it may be in emotional divorces, parents must not play the child against each other. This invariably hurts the child far more than the intended target. The child can become an intermediary for strong emotions and used as the unhealthy sounding board for one spouse lashing out at the other.

Opposites generally attract and subconsciously complement each other in the initial marriage formation, which completes a whole. However, these same delightful differences can undermine a marriage if a couple cannot learn to constructively communicate to resolve conflict. Placing a child in the middle of this "variety gone awry" can be devastating to the young mind and heart. With parents polarized, children have difficulty perceiving the world collectively and can often retreat into a form of fantasy world. Here they create the security that they cannot find in the real world, which has changed around them. Even in divorce, boundaries and cohesion in parenting is vital. Without it, children can develop a form of schizophrenic splitting in terms of dealing with reality. Children of divorce can thus take on one personality in the home of one parent and a completely different one in the other.

Three

Your Marriage Matters
in Parenting

First Things First

Before we launch into ideas about parenting, we feel we must first discuss issues related to what usually precedes "the baby in the baby carriage"—love and marriage. For the sake of effective parenting, those two words, *love* and *marriage*, should become inseparable throughout the years. This chapter discusses ideas on how to do that.

We mentioned earlier that as a society we fail to train parents, unlike doctors and veterinarians, for their important tasks. A successful marriage also takes training, but prospective couples are often too "in love" to see through hormones to a marriage's future. As previously mentioned, some churches and community groups have started formal marriage counseling for couples planning marriage or even those contemplating engagement. The leaders of these groups realize that a good marriage leads to good parenting and a good family. They are trying to ferret out problems in an ounce-of-prevention manner and solve them. This might help the glow of romance endure beyond the honeymoon. For example, some couples never really discuss expectations for major life decisions such as career, education, and children. When conflicts arise over deeply held beliefs, the anger and disappointment from unmet expectations may cause a spouse to think, "I didn't find the right one." Not that premarital counseling should discourage marriage—quite the contrary, it should be the foundation of a strong bond. If problems arise that cannot be worked out, perhaps the union is not meant to be. Realizations such as "I didn't know that he never, ever wanted children" or "She won't support my career goals" are best dealt with in the presence of a marriage counselor or clergy counselor before marriage rather than in the presence of a judge a few months or years after, especially if children are born. We applaud such efforts and hope more prospective nuptials of all ages take advantage of the valuable service. This chapter of our book is an attempt to complement counseling before marriage and especially after.

United We Stand

Your marriage matters in parenting because you must be united as husband and wife to deal with parenting issues such as discipline. When Kimberly sees feuding couples in her office for marriage therapy, she starts with this question: "With all the people in the world out there, how did you two end up together?" Usually, after some blank stares, sniping at each other, and hearing the question rephrased several times, the couples realize that they got together for qualities they are subconsciously seeking to complement, qualities they lacked—the opposites-attract theory. For example, he is shy and reserved; she is outgoing. They sought that quality in the other that they did not possess. However, over many years of quality time together in a marriage, couples usually end up more like each other.

The opposites of attraction, however, often extend to parenting styles. One spouse is usually more permissive or autocratic than the other. Therefore, when disciplining their children, parents can be taken by surprise on how much their parenting styles differ. Children, ever vigilant for opportunities to split the defense, will exploit the real weakness of a disjointed parenting approach. The Mom-says-it's-OK-if-you-do ploy is only one example of the way children take advantage of parents who are not united. Moreover, even if you try the methods in this or other parenting books but are not united, your hit-and-miss efforts will fail by sending conflicting signals to your children. For example, one parent might effectively use the time-out method to deal with a preschooler's anger, whereas the other parent ignores the behavior. The child has "hit the lottery" with one out of two odds. He will play it every time by misbehaving again and again.

So, if you know that you and your spouse have vastly differing views on life and parenting, *do not skip this chapter!* Take the time and effort to make your marriage strong. Even if you think your parenting methods and other life views are similar, use the tools here to keep your marriage strong for even more effective parenting.

The Single Parent

None of what we say in this or other chapters suggests that a single parent cannot be an effective parent. With no polarization of styles, you as a single parent are in charge, and there is no need to consult or collaborate on parenting styles, which, we hope will become more democratic after you read this book. However, we know how hard single parenting can be. Kimberly has counseled hundreds of single parents in her practice and has seen them struggle with the extra parenting load single parenthood brings.

Long Odds

With the divorce rate at an all-time high and many marriages so fragile, it is no wonder that marriage has become a disappearing act: Now you see it, now you don't. The Census Bureau reports that the average marriage in the United States lasts about seven years. There are several reasons to explain marriage fragility these days—two-career family stress, money problems, and the birth of children, just to name a few.

Bruce relates:
We talked about having a large family, but going from three to five kids in one day pushed the stress level in our marriage

to new highs. Having twins was much more difficult than all those years we both spent in graduate school. We used to say that the big adjustment in child rearing was the transition from zero children to one. Now we say it's any number plus two. Some people, not realizing that the kids similar in size are twins, remark, "You're so brave to have them so close together." Right—about four minutes. Since the birth of our twins, we measured our stress level by the "twin-chill factor," which works just like wind chill: Although twins are only two more children, it seems like five. Someone at a Halloween church party voted our van the scariest car—two infant seats.

We're not alone, however. We watched a national news program on the only surviving sextuplets in the United States. The strain on the marriage of the parents of these children was incredible. We were not surprised to learn the divorce rate among couples with multiple births is significantly higher than the national average, which is increasing each year.

Stress

During the first six months of our twins' lives, we found ourselves severely sleep deprived, emotionally drained, and increasingly irritable. When we started blaming each other for the added stress that in actuality our cherished stock split was causing, we admitted the need to regroup and develop a new plan of action to replace our worsening cycle of reactionary anger. Our plan included more date nights and more frequent marriage meetings, discussed later in this chapter. We tried to help each other even more with child duties and housework, discovering that the vacuum cleaner really doesn't care who pushes it. With our twins now five years old, we find the twin-chill factor decreasing as they become more self-sufficient. We seem to have more time for each other, without having to make the time as we had a few years ago, but with a total of six children now, the lessons of keeping a marriage alive are ones we are glad we learned.

Our own marital challenges were obviously induced by the

stress of having twins, in addition to much less spectacular reasons, which all resulted in lack of time and neglect of importance given to the most significant relationship in a family: the marriage relationship. Everything else, including children and careers, comes after the importance of marriage.

After church one Sunday, we met an older man from our congregation. He had noticed our twins causing us obvious stress during church and asked if we were getting enough outside help. We responded that we were surviving with just the two of us. He then said something we will never forget. As the father of twins himself, if he had to do it all over again, he would change only one thing. When the twins were born, he would have done anything—even taken out loans on his home—to hire help for his wife, from whom he was now divorced. Sadly, his scenario is common, as statistics from the national organization of Mothers of Twins Clubs demonstrate. This man found out too late the great importance of his marriage relationship. We had enjoyed spending time together before our double feature started playing. However, with full-time, on-demand breast feeding and overwhelmed with our parental duties, we had neglected the most important relationship—the marital tonic of dating, which we had previously enjoyed. Without our system of functional family democracy, developed after years of research and experience, we too might have become a divorce statistic.

We have learned from our experience and those of others that we water with our time what we want to grow. Marriage relationships need nurturing water, but receive precious few drops after the budding crops get theirs. It is no wonder that marriages with children, especially multiple births, wither and die at a faster rate when starved immediately and so completely after birth.

Three D's of Marital-Parenting Trouble

Division. When Kimberly meets with couples on the verge of separating, often referred by a divorce attorney or a medical doctor, they very often identify the onset of difficulties as the birth of their first child. Many parents, especially mothers, feel compelled to bond exclusively with their needy, fragile infant, never emotionally severing the cord. This lifetime of maternal instinct servitude to children, thereby excluding the spouse, creates marital *division, discord,* and *distance,* which often leads to divorce. Sadly, these couples forget the most important relationship that brought about this wonderful new life.

The marriage relationship that was once nurtured is sometimes neglected after a child is born. On the birth of her first child, a woman becomes a mother, whether a stay-at-home mom or a working mom. It is difficult to understand why people generally don't consider staying at home with children as work. The phraseology must have been developed by someone who has never tried it. In any case, dads become assistants to their now "ex-wives" who tirelessly attend to the multitude of child activities to which they assign themselves.

Discord. As a child grows to become the center of its parents' world, he naturally grows in self-centeredness. The more the child is catered to, the worse the bad habits and negative, selfish behaviors become. The sad irony of the situation is that the more selfish that a child becomes, the more indulgent the parents become. They wrongly believe that they are not doing enough for their child. They dote on the child even more. Parents are reduced to a servile role, without respect from their child and with bad behaviors escalating. When parents finally reach the end of the rope, they sometimes overreact— often with corporal punishment. The parents' guilt from this harsh reaction results in increased servitude, and the negative behaviors surge. This is what we call the *swinging pendulum of parenting:* permissive to autocratic to permissive.

What should have been a union of ideas between spouses on parenting is now a divided mess. As mentioned previously, parental opposites generally attract and subconsciously complement each other, creating the potential for effective parenting. The meaning of synergy is trite but applicable: two parents together will most often make a better decision than one alone. The challenge often then becomes not the parenting issue itself, but reaching a consensus on that parenting issue for a better end result. Single parents, however, may be accustomed to making such decisions without a sounding board.

Without time to resolve parenting issues together, however, parents polarize in their parenting. They retreat to camp on opposite ends of the parenting continuum—autocracy and permissiveness. Without a solid marital foundation and experience in compromising, they refuse to consider the other's parenting viewpoint. The problem with the child is not solved, igniting marital and parenting conflict anew. The cycle creates tremendous discord in an already divided relationship. The child then subconsciously thinks she has won by beating the system, that is, the parents. The "system" is too confused itself to deal with the child. The self-centered child does not realize that discord between parents compromises the family security and love that the child actually yearns for and needs. When parents nurture the child relationship exclusively, the marriage relationship eventually withers without the requisite time and effort to sustain it.

Distance. After years of marital discord, many couples, though still living together physically, are emotionally divorced. These marriages lack the strength necessary to keep them alive. Because most parents are often unaware or too busy to notice that marital discord actually causes their child's misbehavior, the couple doesn't seek counseling for themselves—only for the child with the "problem." Without being united in parenting, or much of anything else, these couples often give up on their child. Sometimes even the school is overwhelmed by the misbehaving child and a referral is made from there.

Kimberly relates:
Many years ago when I was a UCLA intern, I recall working with a family who was referred to the Orange County Child Guidance Center for help with their 10-year-old daughter. Because she had refused to go to school for several days, the school recommended counseling. My supervisor and I asked that the whole family be present for the first session. The situation began to unfold in the office, with the father

autocratically demanding that she go to school or he'd call in the police. Meanwhile, an unkempt, permissive, slouching mother cried in the corner, worried that her daughter was suffering some emotional trauma that was causing her refusal to go to school. Actually, the mother was right—she just didn't know the kind of trauma her daughter was suffering from.

While questioning the family further, we discovered that the father worked late hours as a truck driver and was almost never home. The mother and father hadn't been out together alone in years, and the mother's self-esteem reflected it. Our diagnosis on a family level was that the withdrawn youngest daughter was now reflecting the discord and insecurity in the marital relationship. Not sure that this family would accept our diagnosis immediately, we explained that we believed their daughter's school fears would best be assuaged by first having some bonding time alone with her 16-year-old sister over the weekend. After the youngest daughter agreed to this suggestion, we then asked the parents to go away for the weekend and to return with a plan to best help their daughter realize that she should be in school —her job as a child.

The next session was very interesting. The mother looked ten years younger and was actually wearing make-up. The parents chose to sit on the larger couch next to each other (unlike the previous session), while their youngest daughter excitedly explained that she had attended school the entire week. Both daughters requested more time alone for themselves, which the parents were now eager to give them. The parents seemed to enjoy nurturing their previously dying relationship, which increased their daughter's feeling of security.

Now, when distanced couples come in for counseling or bring their child for treatment, Kimberly always asks the question, "When was the last time you and your spouse spent some quality time alone with each other?" The answer is always the same, "We don't know." Kimberly gives them this advice: For your family's emotional health and ultimate survival, you need to date your mate. This is a novel concept to most people.

Your First Love

Probably the most important thing a father and mother can do for their children is to love each other. The best way of demonstrating that love to children is by expressing to your spouse the affection that brought the children to the family initially. Sadly, many couples have lost the spark they had when they were courting and first married. That excitement for a happy life together is replaced with a boring routine revolving around the lives of their children. It's ironic that children are born as a result of the love a husband and wife feel for each other but that raising children can lead to a painful divorce. Studies have shown that, given the choice, most children prefer to have parents spend more time together than more time with them. It has been demonstrated that when children are able to witness firsthand their parents' priority on dating and romance, the children are more secure and tend to carry that behavior into their own marriage relationships.

It is vital for our children to see happy, loving relationships. In a dysfunctional world, there aren't many to be found. Kimberly frequently asks couples in therapy to think of a couple they respect or admire who seem to have a quality relationship they would like to emulate. Typically, there is a long pause after which one or the other exclaims, "I can't think of any offhand." Is it any wonder couples have so much difficulty when they have no role models, at least none they recognize? It is difficult to copy something that isn't there.

Many children fear that divorce will eventually happen in their family. Children of parents who are emotionally separated figure it's only a matter of time until divorce happens. As you, as a parent, date your spouse, you bring security into the home and set an example for children, which will break the divorce cycle for future generations.

Date Your Mate

When discussing the concept of dating again, many couples are unable to think of what they can do together. Kimberly often asks them to think back to premarital dating to when they shared fun. More blank stares. So she begins probing. Usually, many questions such as "Did you ever take long walks together?" finally jog memories from the past. Then come the excuses for not going out anymore.

- Lack of money
- No baby-sitter
- Limited time available
- Too tired
- Prefer activities with children

It's the last excuse that is the most frustrating. If you're going to spend any time or money, invest in your marriage, for your kid's sake and for yours. It's neither easy nor inexpensive to find a sitter, but the value of time together that adds to a marriage is hard to measure in financial terms. People can make excuses for anything. These kinds of excuses are the cause of the rapid deterioration of many marriages. There is no easy road to a strong marriage, but if couples are willing to invest, the rewards for the entire family are well worth it.

What follows are some creative dating ideas for you and your spouse to enjoy. Some are neither expensive nor particularly time consuming. Others take effort that will undoubtedly pay off. Try to remember some of your favorite dates in the past or find something creative from the list below.

- Have breakfast while watching a sunrise together
- View a sunset while taking a walk hand in hand
- Tour a free museum
- Visit an art gallery and pack a lunch
- Picnic near a pond; bring two fishing poles
- Send your spouse a love letter; list the reasons that you married him or her
- Give your spouse a massage
- Rent a classic romance and watch it while cuddling
- Take a canoe ride together

- Swim in the moonlight
- Have a romantic dinner for two while the kids view a new video
- Review old photo albums while picnicking at a park
- Take a getaway over a long weekend
- Ask your spouse out for a date by phone from work
- Go kite flying at the beach
- Build a fire; reminisce about your first date
- Take a bubble bath together
- Perfume new satin bedsheets
- Serve your spouse breakfast in bed
- Share a shake or other dessert—two spoons
- Write the story of how you both met; have it bound for your children
- Write a poem for each other
- Do something your spouse loves to do; then trade off
- Draw a floor plan of your dream house together
- Make a list of your spouse's best qualities and exchange lists—keep it for future reference

Going on a date each week provides the preventive care marriages need to survive. We find that our kids not only don't mind our dates, but actually look forward to them. Your children will thank you for the increased strength of your relationship, which makes your parenting job a little easier.

Bruce relates:

When I was 19 years old, I served as a missionary for the Church of Jesus Christ of Latter-day Saints for two years in Japan. All of us were assigned companions with whom to live and carry out the missionary work. One of the requirements from the church administrators was called companion inventory. Each week, we as companions were asked to sit down together and talk about our relationship—how things were going, if one was doing anything to upset the other, what plans we had for the missionary work. Rather than a mutual gripe session—"Well, you burned the rice!"—I discovered that these sessions built respect and trust for one another like nothing else. We found ourselves expressing genuine concern for each other's emotional welfare, since our experiences in a land far from home were inextricably linked. It's hard to imagine better training for a marriage relationship than the character-developing experience of getting along with an assigned companion. We were transferred and reassigned a new companion typically after three or four months of service together. When I was released as a missionary, I remember thinking that bringing these companion inventories into my marriage would be a good idea. They've turned out to be more important to a relationship in which there are no transfers!

Marriage Meetings

Marriage meetings are crucial to keep the lines of communication open between spouses. Meeting on the run to quickly converse on child pick-up and drop-off for the day does not qualify. Issues and feelings should be discussed informally—daily if possible—preferably, at a time when you can both be alone and can sit close enough to touch each other. Such circumstances are more conducive to cooperation and problem solving than arguing. Predetermined, agreed-upon bedtimes for children that are enforced can afford you the time to be alone.

At least once a week take a minimum of forty minutes for your marriage meeting—perhaps after or during your weekly date night. We found that when our twins were born, our weekly formal meeting became almost nightly. We discussed the stresses of the day, attempted to resolve the constant challenges that arose, and tried to always point out the positive aspects of our relationship and family. Also, we encouraged each other and focused on the positive, creating a healthy relationship in the midst of much pressure. We found that we were more stressed during this time than at any other time in our married life.

Most couples find it difficult to make time to discuss issues together. However, it is extremely effective in bonding couples. During marriage meetings, weekly date nights can be discussed and planned for the upcoming week. Naturally, both of these exercises help cut down on marriage therapy bills as well. Many couples find it helpful to have their couple marriage meeting prior to the family meeting to reach agreement on issues that might divide them while holding the family meeting with the children. Ideas on how to stop negative behaviors can be discussed as well as plans for family fun. Family fun should come second to couple fun.

Four

Birth Order and Behavior

OK—you've made your marriage strong, you are united in your parenting approach. Now you've decided to have children. You should know that each child perceives the world based on his or her ordinal position in the family and the parental treatment accordingly. The oldest child in the family sees the world much differently than the youngest. And both siblings may be treated quite differently by their parents.

Kimberly has always had an interest in birth order and its effects on the family. In therapy work with children and families, it can be helpful to change family perceptions when issues of birth order make things difficult for the family. Each ordinal position, first, second, third, or later, has its own typical personality traits and attitudes. Spacing and gender of the children also play an important role. A third child born eight years after the second can actually act more like an only child rather than the second born. Depending on her birth order, a girl born into a family of four boys can be very different than a female born into a family of four other girls. An only girl is often treated as Daddy's little girl by her father. Also, a mother may treat an only girl with many brothers special because the daughter is the only other female. Kimberly often hears brothers of one-daughter families recount memories such as, "She got away with everything."

The Burden of the Firstborn

As early as 1918, psychology pioneer Alfred Adler believed there was a correlation between birth order and personality. On the basis of his clinical observations, Adler described firstborns as more achievement-oriented than later born children and more sensitive to the wishes of the parents and more willing to conform to authority in general. He observed that firstborns were more comfortable with adult peers, because the firstborn, as the only child in a family for a period of time, interacts exclusively with adults in the form of his parents.

Until the birth of the second child, firstborns are the center of attention. When the second child arrives, the first often feels left out and unimportant. When Kimberly teaches parenting classes or works with families specifically dealing with dethronement issues, she often asks mothers to picture their husbands returning home from a business trip with another woman, whom he introduces as his second wife. Imagine his confusion when his first wife becomes angry. His explanation could be, "You are such a great wife, I figured I'd just have another one." This is often how the pampered firstborn child feels when informed that another child is on the way.

Resentment, however, is not the reaction of all firstborn children. Kimberly has a friend who grew up on a farm as a firstborn. At age four years, she greatly anticipated the birth of her sibling. She recalls the eager anticipation of having a playmate and someone to share in the family chores. It was her responsibility to throw feed to the chickens and corn to the milk cow—her sibling would provide companionship and help in these tasks.

It is important for parents to present the news of the impending arrival in such a way that the firstborn can be excited and look forward to a sibling's birth. Discussion on how happy the family will be with another child helps. The transition need not be painful if you prepare ahead of time.

At the birth, one way of establishing immediate bonding between the baby and an older sibling is buying a special gift for the baby to give to its sibling. Carefully choose a gift that the older child would really prize. Take the gift with you to the hospital in anticipation of your firstborn's visit. The older sibling will feel that the baby can't be all bad if it comes into the world bearing gifts! Remember, your eldest hasn't seen her mom for a few days and will expect all of her mom's attention—just as always.

The sibling gift idea has been used with much success by clients Kimberly has worked with over the years and even with our own children. Incredibly, all our older children, when asked, still remember the gifts each baby gave them at the hospital. This tradition created special bonding memories for them and a much more pleasurable hospital visit for us all around.

The oldest child in a family is just that—older and definitely more responsible, at least for a number of years. Therefore, the firstborn has special privileges the baby won't have. While the mother is feeding the baby or changing a diaper, the firstborn can prepare his own meal from a food shelf stocked with his favorite nutritious foods, which can significantly cut down on attention-getting behaviors that often surface at baby's feeding time. The child feels a sense of accomplishment the child feels when such a rite of passage is fulfilled.

Potty training is another rite. We felt it was time to train one of our toddlers when he came up to us wearing a dirty diaper, handed us a clean one, and said, "Put this on." We always find it interesting when second-time parents fear that the firstborn's potty training efforts will grind to a halt when the new baby arrives. The only reason that this can and does happen is self-fulfilling prophecy. If you assume your child will regress, he or she often does. Guilt and lowered expectations from parents are internalized by the child. Regression need not occur if the firstborn is made to feel more responsible and, therefore, doesn't need diapers like the baby. Because money isn't spent on diapers for the older child, the firstborn should have special privileges like Happy Meals at McDonald's, ice pops, and other treats the baby can't and doesn't yet enjoy. Carefully explaining this to the firstborn will make the transition much easier. Don't assume the worst. Expect the best by planning for it before the baby's arrival.

Other ideas include a new big kid bed for easier transition from the crib. Big boy or girl panties embossed with a favorite character are also fun and represent a significant rite of passage. While Bruce was in graduate school in Boston, our second-born was just days away from arrival. Kimberly's mother had come from California to help following the birth of our son, and help she did. We had just started potty training our two-and-a-half-year-old daughter. Not only was our daughter potty trained when we returned home from the hospital with our new son, but she had visited her mother and the baby at the hospital in her new big girl panties from Grandma Sharon. Our daughter never looked back, having given her diapers to her baby brother. This was not done through spanking or coercion of any form. She just thought it would be cool to be a big sister with all that goes with her new family status.

Not surprisingly, studies have shown that firstborn children suffering from dethronement are frequently known to fight for their mother's now divided attention. In doing so, they tend to demand the rights and the prerogatives of being first. They seem to want to maintain power and authority over younger siblings and fear they will lose their rightful place if they relax their efforts. Often if the first child cannot maintain his supreme position through positive behavior, he may attempt to get attention in a negative way.

Kimberly relates:

I was treating a 15-year-old adolescent at a local psychiatric hospital. The youth had attempted suicide at school by slashing his wrists with a razor blade. After three days in the psychiatric hospital, he had disclosed no apparent reason for the suicide attempt. In our first meeting, I asked the young man to tell me his first recollections as a child. He stared at the floor and with grit teeth stated, "I remember when I was four, my mom rocking my sister and nursing her and I hated them."

Later, I discussed the mother's relationship with her son.

She stated that after the birth of her daughter, her son would not allow the mother to touch him and he became severely depressed. Other than the birth of the sister, the young man's life had none of the usual life stressors for children, such as divorce or deaths in the family, or frequent moves. This youth had not progressed developmentally nor emotionally subsequent to the birth of his sister. No one had recognized this or made any attempt to help him vent his dethronement and discouragement during the ensuing ten or eleven years. Finally, the resentment and anger erupted in a suicide attempt.

Sadly, this youth hadn't seen the birth of his sister in a positive light. It was obvious from subsequent meetings that his mother found life's responsibilities overwhelming. Adjusting to motherhood was a huge task itself, let alone finding ways of helping her son make a successful transition. She could have eased her own burden by allowing her son, then three years old, to help with the care of his new sister as her big brother. He could have helped bathe her or even feed her. The ideas suggested above could have aided with further bonding between the baby and the dethroned firstborn. Preparation is the key.

Another issue in this family was spousal neglect. The mother in the case example, like many other mothers, became enthralled with the baby and devoted herself solely to the care of her baby, unable to give attention to anyone else, which happens in many families when children enter the picture. Fathers can also feel dethroned and may seek to meet their emotional needs elsewhere. Many divorces occur each year for just such reasons, as discussed in the chapter "Your Marriage Matters in Parenting."

The suicidal youth could also have been reacting to the stressful, weakened marriage. The spousal relationship is key to the emotional health of children and to the success or failure of the entire family. After all, who came first, the couple or the children? Parents often forget.

The Pressure to Achieve

Researchers have discovered that parents often continue to press firstborns throughout their lives for greater achievement and optimal performance. The groundwork begins with the adult stimulation focused on the firstborn during the only-child period. By becoming adult-oriented and internalizing adult standards for intellectual performance and achievement at an early age, firstborns can undergo more stress and anxiety than later borns.

Firstborn children also tend to accept responsibility for the younger children even after the younger children can and should care for themselves. The age grading or hierarchical awarding of status and power as a function of age occurs universally in families, with long-lasting significance. When this imbalance continues too long, the younger children typically grow up feeling less powerful than the older siblings, and the firstborn becomes dominant in sibling interactions. Parents can allow all children to be responsible by not awarding power based only on age. When parents leave the home, all children can assume responsibility for their own behavior and be rewarded accordingly (paid for baby-sitting themselves, basically). Although a legal-aged baby-sitter may be present, children can and should take responsibility for themselves.

At one of our family meetings years ago, we initiated a plan with our children. We noticed a problem after experiencing some negative dominance by the older siblings when we left home for weekly date nights. At the meeting, we expressed our hope that all the children could be responsible for themselves while we were gone—if they were old enough to understand the meaning of self-reliance, they could take charge of themselves. We would pay them if they assumed that self-responsibility. If not, they would need to pay the baby-sitter to supervise them. They accepted our plan, and the hierarchical class-rating system, at least for baby-sitting, was a thing of the past.

Other research shows that firstborns who achieve their goals without parent pressure have more pride in themselves and have higher self-esteem. They excel because they want to, not just because they are told to. To raise responsible children, parents should give the firstborn a break by delegating duties to the younger children. The firstborn can then volunteer to help, rather than being obligated. Perhaps parents could appoint occasionally the second-born to baby-sit the younger children.

Another way of sharing responsibilities in the family is by allowing each child an opportunity to chair a weekly family meeting and to make assignments. Try to rotate the responsibility of choosing the dessert after meetings. Family members can also take turns choosing family weekend activities as well. Families in which all children are expected to meet similar standards and share responsibilities will likely have a more evenly distributed achievement orientation and level of self-esteem, which contrasts the stereotypical domineering firstborn and the introverted second born or last born.

The Second Born's Game of Catch-Up

The child in the second birth order position is continually confronted with someone who is always a step ahead. The second born may become discouraged and display inadequacy because of the inability to keep up with the older sibling. For better or worse, this often causes the second born to oppose the firstborn sibling in an attempt to be different and to establish individual identity. The problem is compounded when parents label and compare the second born and later born children to the firstborn child. If the firstborn is achievement oriented and parents extol this virtue to the second born, he will often become an underachiever just to be contrary. The second born can be more outgoing or less, depending on the characteristics of the older sibling and to what degree the firstborn is praised by the parents. Naturally, with most families in the United States composed of two children, the comparison becomes even more frequent. Parents of two children should be extra vigilant in avoiding unhealthy comparisons.

Kimberly recalls working with a child who was constantly compared to his older sibling. There was even a wall in the family room dedicated to trophies and achievements of the two children. Though intended to stimulate improvement, it only increased depression in the less achievement-oriented child. A well-meaning parent gesture was actually harassment for the younger child. Therefore, Kimberly uses only noncompetitive games with the children she works with. These games encourage cooperation among siblings and family members in general. In these games, you only win if everyone wins. You work together as a group to achieve all goals. She has been accused of not preparing children, including our own, for the competitive society in which they will ultimately live. The response is that there is enough competition in society as it is—children are forced to compete from the first day they walk into a school classroom. What prepares them best, however, is the cooperation and love that should be emphasized in the home.

The Middle-Child Syndrome

When a third child enters the family, the second child becomes a middle child, who often feels emotionally squeezed and confused, having neither the rights of the oldest nor the indulgence of the baby. Without direction and attention, the middle child may believe that life is unfair or may try to overcome the disadvantaged position with negative, attention-getting behavior. The middle child is often overly concerned with fairness and conformance. This child desperately needs to establish identity and to develop special abilities early in life to avoid loss of self-esteem, which frequently occurs when the child feels there is nothing special or unique about being middle born.

Just recently, our third born of six made a profound statement while Kimberly was tucking him into bed after his special story time. He said, "You know, I'm a middle child in our family!" After she said, "That's right!" she asked what he thought about that. He said, "Not much really, someone just told me that at school today." He had never really thought of himself as a middle born before, he just thought of himself as our eight-year-old son who finally turned old enough to play football, the sport he has waited his entire life to play. Although we know the dangers of this high contact sport, we feel it is important for our son to choose for himself. Since football is his passion, Bruce is coaching to share special time with our son, for as long as he wants to continue playing.

To grow and mature successfully, every child must establish her own style and a drive for work. It is often a challenge for the middle born however, prompting one writer to label this child "the human sandwich." Says psychologist and birth order expert Arnstein: "The middle child has a less-defined role in relation to parents as well as to the family. Middle born children must often struggle harder in some families to strengthen their shaky sense of identity." This may explain the finding of R.J. Gallagher and Emory Cowen, prominent child psychologists, that middle borns are more predisposed to cope with problems by resorting to shy or anxious behaviors. It is so important therefore not to label children when these behaviors are manifested. Never say to others, "Oh, she's just shy" or "She won't answer you!" This stifles emotional growth and retards a child's progress when he could move ahead if encouraged. A withdrawn child who gets help in choosing appropriate extracurricular activities will get outside herself in an effort to find herself.

It has also been found that more middle borns exhibit learning problems in school because of lack of identity and belief in them-selves. Parents should not use this as an excuse, but should maintain the same expectations of effort for their middle born child as for any of their other children. Children will rise to the level of expectations of their parents and others. They need your belief in them when they have difficulty at times believing in themselves. Middle children who are able to establish identity are more easygoing than other siblings. Most middle children have increased empathy for the underdog, with whom they identify. They are most often the peacemakers, and oth-ers tend to seek them out for sympathy and understanding.

The Last Born's Special Challenges

Adler wrote that the "youngest child remains forever the baby of the family." As the last born, these children can never be dethroned, and do remain, in some ways, always special. The youngest child runs a high risk of being pampered and spoiled because the older siblings are so available. If they offer help too readily, the youngest child might expect others to solve all of his problems, in which case the child has no need to become independent.

Kimberly relates:

Some years ago, I was working with a large family with six siblings. The youngest boy, Nathan, three-and-one-half years old, was identified by the other family members as the "problem." According to his mother, Nathan would throw temper tantrums when he could not get his way; he refused to be potty trained and he would not communicate with his parents except through his older siblings. His siblings claimed that they would frequently speak for Nathan because they could understand his baby talk when adults could not. While in therapy with the entire family, questioning directed to Nathan would frequently be answered by older siblings, indicative of what typically occurred at home. As therapist, I asked Nathan if this happens often—his family members speaking for him. He nodded affirmatively. I reframed the problem by pointing out that when other family members speak for Nathan, he has no need to spend energy to speak for himself. This family had enabled Nathan's tendency not to speak, which was bringing him special attention and power in the family. It continued to delay his development before intervention.

The youngest child is often inclined to take advantage of her special position by becoming a tyrant. The youngest can also demand special attention by being the cutest, most pleasant, weakest, or most awkward—all that a child can be by virtue of being the youngest. If discouraged, the youngest child may often seek a place in the family by playing the clown or by openly rebelling in an attempt to take power or attention from older siblings. Many youngest children choose to become excessively achievement oriented to outdo everyone ahead of them and to gain recognition. They often adopt the mistaken idea that they must overachieve to belong. They can become adults who are constantly overachieving, still attempting to assert their significance in the family.

> Bruce relates:
>
> *I was the youngest of four; Kimberly was the oldest of two. I like to tease her that I read the individuals that did all of those studies that show firstborns to be more achievement oriented, intelligent, and charming are mostly first-borns! As the youngest, I do recall trying to play a sort of catch-up diplomat, since there were four children in my family, three of whom were older and more experienced than I was. On one of our first dates, I remember asking Kimberly, "Do you have any pets?" She responded, "Sure— a little brother."*

The Only Child

Children with no siblings live their formative years among adults who are mature and more capable. Only children often develop a distinctive style that ensures them a place with adults. These children may become charming, verbal, and intelligent, or, perhaps to receive special attention, shy and helpless. As adults, they may feel they are entitled to have their own way because they have grown up having it. Parents of an only child need to understand the child's unique issues and establish appropriate parent-child boundaries and expectations.

Walter Toman, a famous birth order theorist, proposes in his family constellation theory that the role a person had in early familial relationships carries over into adult relationships. However, it is important to note that the positions in the family constellation only influence an individual's personality development and do not necessarily determine it.

Other researchers have concluded that it is common for pregnant mothers to identify with a baby in the same ordinal position as hers in her family of origin. A woman whose ordinal position is second and who readily identifies with her second child inside her womb may view the firstborn as a representation of her older sibling. Depending on her childhood relationship with the older sibling, the mother may experience a repetition of her own sibling relationship, with all its emotional content.

The different approaches by caretakers toward the firstborn and the second born will naturally have an impact on the child's capacities and role in future psychosocial relationships. Caretakers, however, should not feel solely responsible for the resulting personality of a child. Other environmental factors, such as the number of siblings or lack of them, can have a profound effect on a child's development.

Each child has her own perception of her position in the family and can make decisions accordingly. Parents, however, can affect their children's perceptions of their position in the family by understanding the influence of ordinal position. They can encourage uniqueness, share responsibility among siblings, avoid comparisons, stifle competition, and understand the goals of each child's misbehavior and respond appropriately without overreacting. The topic of fostering cooperation without competition is a focus of the next chapter, "Encouraging Children."

Five

Encouraging Children

onstructive Criticism: A Contradiction in Terms
Ineffective methods of child rearing focus on maintaining dependency, promoting competition with siblings and others, overprotection, and setting unrealistic standards for children. These techniques produce discouraged children as discussed earlier. Parents must avoid making negative comments. Dr. John Lund in his best-selling book *Avoiding Emotional Divorce* explains that constructive criticism is a complete contradiction of terms. Constructive means to build up, whereas criticism means to tear down. All forms of criticism are discouraging and despite the hope of parents, will not change behavior for the better. Criticism is like a cancer that eats away at a child's self-concept. Consequences for behavior, whether negative or positive, are vital for responsible parenting and are different from criticism.

To help children build feelings of self-esteem, you may need to change your usual style of communicating and parenting. Instead of dwelling on mistakes, point out the children's successes. Encourage positive behaviors through democratic parenting styles. The following chart will help you differentiate between autocratic and democratic motivation techniques in parenting.

TECHNIQUES OF MOTIVATING CHILDREN

Autocratic Parenting	*Democratic Parenting*
Parents reward child, based on arbitrary and extrinsic standards.	Parents influence child through cooperative discipline and encouragement.
Parents demand obedience through control.	Parents permit choices; child becomes more resourceful and responsible.
Parents display superiority by pitying, spoiling, and overprotecting child.	Parents give child same respect as shown adults; child can trust others.
Parents demand perfection; child lacks self-esteem, excessively fears disapproval from others.	Parents tolerate child making mistakes; child learns to try new experiences.
Parents feel child owes them; child feels exploited and exploits others; nontrusting.	Parents and child share responsibilities; not ruled by guilt; child ultimately respects others and self.

A former client of Kimberly's felt it was time for her 5-year-old daughter to dress herself to increase responsibility and gain independence. Despite this goal, each day the mother arranged her daughter's clothing for her and criticized her daughter's initial efforts to dress herself. The mother was concerned with what others would think about her daughter's shoes on the wrong feet and shirt not tucked in. When her daughter wanted to choose her own outfits, the mother, perceiving this as a form of rebellion, refused. After several months, the mother did allow her daughter to dress herself, but enforced strict guidelines on the acceptable combination of clothes. Outfits that didn't match were forbidden.

In therapy, the mother was taught the importance of encouraging the daughter's attempts at dressing herself by focusing on the task at hand, not others' criticism. There was no reason a child of that age could not choose her own clothing, within reasonable limits. By deciding on her own, the daughter could gradually learn what goes together, as opposed to relying on the mother to make decisions for her. Making independent choices establishes a pattern of self-reliance for the future.

When the child had trouble getting her shirt over her head, the mother could say, "You're getting it—now slide it a little to the left—that's the way." Eventually, the clothing issue was settled in a way that kept both the daughter and mother's self-esteem intact.

The Language of Encouragement

Described above is the language of encouragement, which can be a foreign language to some of us, since we might not have experienced it in our own homes. Encouragement requires parents to stop using damaging negative comments about their children. When children do misbehave, parents can clearly express their own feelings of disapproval of the behavior but yet approval of the child. Accepting the child while rejecting a particular behavior is crucial to encouragement. It separates the deed from the doer and keeps self-esteem from dissolving into discouragement. Love should never be withheld because a child has misbehaved or disappointed the parent. The child needs to experience unconditional love and encouragement. Even a misbehaving child can be encouraged, as illustrated in the following example. "Susie, as we discussed earlier, you have chosen not to have a snack today because you left a mess yesterday. I bet tomorrow you'll remember to clean up at snack time." Notice the focus is on the deed, not the doer. The daughter can feel that her mom believes in her, which should encourage cooperation at snack time the next day.

In another example, parents point out the one C on a report card and fail to comment on the B's and A's. When we accept our children unconditionally when they are making their best effort, we build their confidence and give them the courage to try. In Japan, the competition to get into the best colleges is quite keen. After completing high school, most students study in private courses for at least a year to prepare for the entrance exam, which determines the college a student will attend. Sadly, the suicide rate for this age group spikes sharply upward each year when the results of the exam are announced. This tragic group of Japanese teens have their self-concept based entirely on the approval of parents and others. They feel totally worthless when they don't measure up.

When children receive praise from parents for only the best grades, they can become depressed with any grade lower than an A. Emphasizing a child's shortcomings or praising only superachievements can actually have the opposite of the intended effect. Instead of instilling confidence, parents end deflating the child's ego. If the child achieves anything less than first prize, he feels like a failure.

Constructive Encouragement versus Damaging Praise

Next we consider encouragement versus praise. More than semantics, the difference between the two is crucial to raising responsible children. Praise means talking positively only when the child achieves what the parent considers success. Subconsciously, praise can be a control measure. To earn praise, parents often feel that the child must please them or meet their standards. The meaning, however unintended, is "I love you only when ..." The child cannot help but conclude that he must achieve the parents' standards to be worthy of their love. Please or Perish is the message sent to the child. Rather than encourage, praise can discourage because it is based on competition—outdoing others or achieving someone else's goals. One of life's hard lessons is that someone will always be smarter, faster, more beautiful, talented, but, gladly never all of the above. Nobody's the best at everything they attempt. Children constantly need encouragement to develop their innate talents, regardless of instant success. They will find their own natural strengths and weaknesses. Children cannot succeed unless they believe in themselves and know that their parents believe in them, too.

Encouragement recognizes effort and improvement and focuses on children's assets and contributions to the democratic family. Many of our nation's problems rooted in materialism result from the focus on being the best at all cost. We praise only the richest, fastest, smartest, sexiest, without regard to the personal gain that was achieved at the expense of others. "Greed is good" went the famous line from the movie *Wall Street* several years ago.

Often young boys are brought to therapy with low self-esteem. When no apparent family stressor can be identified, the discouragement often stems from an ego-deflating sports experience. Children in competitive team sports are sometimes devastated by their treatment from coaches and peers. Typically, coaches of children ironically rely on criticism and praise in attempts to drive their teams onto esteem-building victory. If coaches and parents do not keep games in perspective, however, the result is lower self-esteem.

The influence of organized team sports on a child's life, however, can be positive. Cooperation, hard work, and discipline are lessons children can learn in a positive, healthy setting. Winning can be fun, but only one team wins a contest. Children must also learn that playing the game is just as much fun, and that losing, while not as much fun, can be handled with dignity and the proper perspective.

Many winning professional team coaches have adopted the autocratic, tyrannical style, but on a little-league level, this is hardly appropriate. We have even encountered little-league sports with the motto Win or Die. Coaches and parents who live by this motto even display it on their team shirts, forgoing a healthy family life by supporting excessive practices to win at all costs. Luckily, at the high school and collegiate level, many successful coaches have employed a more encouraging and balanced approach.

In a parenting class taught by Kimberly a few years ago, a member of the class brought in a book on the most successful high school and college coaches of the decade. The recurrent theme of the book was that these coaches led their teams to success by encouraging the players' efforts to improve and showing appreciation for individual contributions that resulted in scoring, not the final score itself. They trusted team members to evaluate and improve themselves.

> Bruce relates:
> *I remember in college seeing one of these collections of motivational speakers coming through town. John Wooden, the most successful coach in collegiate basketball history, spoke to the group seated in a large arena. He was clearly uncomfortable with the hype of the typical go-get-'em speakers. I remember him saying, "I never talked of winning with my UCLA players—not even in the big games. I talked of only doing our best."*

We need to encourage our children to do their best at whatever they attempt. This alone will promote greater self-esteem, which will allow them not only to survive but to be successful in this all-too-competitive world.

Specific words and labels: To develop an encouraging vocabulary, eliminate value-laden words such as *good, great,* and *bad.* These words express our values and opinions and do not help children to believe in themselves. The following groups of phrases can help resolve that problem.

A.   Focusing on a child's contributions to the family:
*   *Thanks—that helped me a lot.*
*   *I really appreciated _____, because it made our home run more smoothly.*
*   *I really need your help doing_____.*
*   *I've noticed you have a skill in _____. Would you do that for the family?*

B.   Showing encouragement and confidence in the discouraged child:

- *Knowing your capabilities, I'm sure you'll do fine.*
- *You can do it.*
- *I have confidence in your judgment.*
- *That seems like a rough one now, but I'm sure you'll work it out.*
- *I bet you'll figure it out.*

C. Recognizing your child's effort and improvement no matter how small:
- *It looks as if you really worked hard on that.*
- *You seemed to have spent a lot of time thinking that through.*
- *I can see that you are moving right along on that project.*
- *Look at the progress you've made in _____. (Be specific)*
- *I feel you're improving in_____. (Be specific)*
- *You may not feel that you've reached your goal, but look how far you've come.*

D. Conveying unconditional acceptance and love:
- *I like the way you handled that situation.*
- *I like the way you tackled your problems.*
- *I'm glad you enjoy learning.*
- *I'm glad you are pleased with it. (Note: Instead of "good job!")*
- *Since you're not satisfied, what do you think you would like to do more?*
- *It looks as if you enjoyed that.*
- *How do you feel about it?*

In short, encouragement focuses on recognizing effort and improvement instead of receiving praise for achievement only. Encouraging words express faith in children so that they believe in themselves. Encouragement verifies appreciation and acceptance of children just as they are, not as they could be. Lastly, encouragement focuses on children's contributions and on the positive aspects of their behavior, which decreases discouragement when children aren't the best.

Cooperation versus Competition

A few years ago, our children's elementary school held an awards ceremony. Approximately one out of thirty children received recognition for outstanding academic achievement or good citizenship. Our daughter noticed that after the ceremony, a few children were crying, disappointed in not being a winner chosen from among their classmates. During the ceremony, other children who were not recognized seemed to feel dejected that their efforts were not acknowledged. The school most likely had the best of intentions, as schools have for decades, by recognizing children who achieve. The other children, however, are not encouraged to do better during the coming months. Life is not one competitive Academy Awards ceremony after the other. Competition should not be a daily, constant pressure on children at school nor especially in the home.

Mrs. Anderson tries to instill the importance of attaining good grades in her children. She sets up her firstborn as a model student in the eyes of the other children and then wonders aloud why the younger siblings don't live up to the standards of the firstborn. Not surprisingly, the other children continually resent the older child, and unhealthy competition is the rule around the house. Comparing and labeling children discourages them.

Another problem in extremely competitive families is tattling. Children use tattling to get even with another sibling or to appear better than the others. To achieve cooperation in a family of tattlers, parents must ignore the tattling. Children will learn how to work things out for themselves when they are no longer able to use the weapon of parents against their siblings. When the negative tattling behavior is ignored, it will be replaced by positive cooperation. Dangerous situations are, of course, different, and children should be taught that it's appropriate to inform parents when someone is doing something harmful. If a child is involved in a harmful activity, try to remedy the situation, not throttle the offender. Otherwise, the dangerous act may be repeated as a way to involve the parent or to get even with a sibling.

Encourage Your Children Through Love

One of our favorite quotes is in a small frame on the wall leading to the bedrooms of our six children. It reads, "Children that deserve love the least need it the most." When our children are in the negative mode and choose one or more of the goals of bad behavior, we as parents constantly remind each other of this quote because we often feel less inclined to show love when they choose to misbehave. As adults, during most of the time we spend in the world, we are not encouraged to overcome our shortcomings and faults, particularly in a work setting. Unfortunately, in our homes, it follows that parents generally dwell on the negative in the belief that it will help their children improve.

In our home, we are constantly saying to our children, "Regardless of what you chose to do, we still love you." Even though we must follow through with the appropriate consequence for their chosen behavior, we will always love them. We remind them that we discipline them because we love them. One of our children's favorite bedtime story books is entitled *Love You Forever* by Robert Munsch. In the book, the little boy's mother comes into his room to cradle him nightly despite negative behaviors during the day. He grows up feeling valued and loved and reciprocates his mother's love and respect in her aging years.

Twelve Ways of Expressing Love to Children

1. *Time.* Nothing can replace time with your children—not money, gifts, or even occasional trips. The argument that quality time can compensate for a lack of quantity is seriously flawed—in fact, it's a myth. Children at a young age do not know the difference. Either the parent is there or not. Granted, a dozing, TV-watching parent is not as influential as an actively involved one. Five minutes of quality time, however, should not be an excuse for neglecting the children the rest of the evening. Children need to have special regular time with their parents—time they can count on and anticipate. If you make your children and family your top priority, friends, job, or out-

side interests will not receive more of your time than is reasonably necessary.

Whatever happened to eating together as a family? It might require advance preparation for a dinner together. It might mean the kids help in preparing a meal, or maybe you order pizza once in a while. Even with pizza, however, we try not to stand around wolfing it down, but sit down as we would for a regular meal, say a blessing on the food, and pass the plates. We have found that whatever sacrifices we make to spend time together pays off in immeasurable dividends.

Bedtime can be a special time for parent and child. We have a routine of stories, snuggles, songs, and sharing with each child. If other children interrupt, we say, "This is ———'s and my time together. You and I will be together at the time we agreed upon." Our children use this time to share the events of their day. Parents at bedtime should focus on active listening. We often start the discussion by asking for one happy thing about the day and one sad thing. In addition to weekly family meetings and fun time together, we try to take each child on a special date for one-on-one time, which they have come to treasure.

2. "I Love You." Express this sentiment in words at least once each day with hugs, kisses, smiles, approving pats, and affirming nods. Showing your children every day that you love them, especially spontaneously, is very important. Write your children love notes in lunch boxes, under pillows, or on dressers. While away on a trip, record a message on a cassette tape or write a letter saying how glad you are that she is your child. On a ten-day second honeymoon abroad, we left presents (candy bars, small toys) and dated notes for each child as reminders of our love. It gave the children something to look forward to each day. Also, a calendar with stickers helped the time pass more quickly and allowed them to anticipate our return.

3. "Thank you." Show daily appreciation for each child and his special contributions. "I appreciate how you set the table without even being asked, it sure makes our home run smoother—thanks!" "Your smile definitely brightens my day. I sure enjoy seeing it!" How often do we nag, criticize, and complain about minor omissions rather than encourage positive behavior? It's no wonder kids are so discouraged.

4. Set an example. Model the high standards and the attitudes and expectations you believe in. Hypocrisy only breeds rebellion and discouragement. In our favorite antidrug commercial, an angry father asks his son where he learned to do drugs. "From you," the son replies. Be a loving example to your children by speaking words that edify and encourage. Children will generally replicate attitudes of their parents. If you are gloomy and dissatisfied with life, your child may adopt your outlook. Since children mirror our emotions, we should not be too shocked hearing complaints from them if we were grumbling hours before. Be patient and kind even when you don't feel like it—perhaps your children will learn to do the same.

5. Be friendly. Show interest without preaching. A friend shares and listens without judgment. Friends seek to understand. "You seem troubled ... do you want to talk?" Try to see the world from your child's vantage point. Avoid advice-giving; children often have more insight into their own lives than their parents do. Blanket statements and advice, although well-intended, do not help the child learn to weigh options and make decisions on his own. Allowing children to make decisions based on their own judgment encourages them to learn.

6. Use humor. Often children respond well to a wink, a pun, or a laugh at oneself. In addition to lightening up a difficult situation, humor enables us to learn from our mistakes. We need to have the courage as parents to accept imperfection in ourselves and others. As a result, children will learn that mistakes can be learning tools, not a cause for shame. In our family, we frequently laugh at ourselves as parents when we make silly mistakes, such as forgetting things, spilling things. We find that when we do this our children better accept their own attempts at adulthood. Our children have learned that when life gets too stressful, find humor.

7. Recognize effort and improvement. As discussed earlier, praise is discouraging because it compares the child against some external standard. Recognizing your child's effort encourages him or her to continue to try. Identify times when your child's improvement in a certain area is noticeable, and verbally recognize achievements. Respond enthusiastically to all successes, no matter how small. This will help your child feel self-confident even if she wasn't "the best" at a given task or function.

8. Trust. Have faith in your children and accept them so they can in turn believe in themselves. Children who feel trusted become trustworthy. Children who are not trusted live up (or *down*) to that expectation.

9. Respect. Never discuss your child negatively with others in front of your child. This shows a complete lack of respect and destroys parent-child relationships. Encourage and show appreciation for your child in front of others, and he will live up to the faith you have in him. It seems that our children constantly bring our attention to other parents who put down their children both in front of the children and behind their children's backs. Our own children ask, "Do you do that, too?'"

Parents often complain that their children do not respect them. Respect is earned by showing respect to others. Nagging, yelling, hitting, talking down, overdoing for children, following double standards—all show lack of respect.

10. Mind your own business. Children tend to rebel against parents who interfere by trying to solve their problems, such as a disagreement with a friend at school. Within certain reasonable guidelines, children need wide latitude in attending to their own concerns and interests. Making decisions for themselves is an important and vital skill that must be learned if children are to assume roles as responsible adults. You will learn in later chapters to rely on natural and logical consequences to help your children become responsible and independent by learning from their own mistakes.

11. Encourage and support their interests. As previously mentioned, we let our son pursue his passion for playing football and will let him continue for as long as he would like. In fact, Bruce helps coach the team to make it more of a father-son experience. He also helps coach our older son's basketball team. One of our daughter's strengths is creative thinking, and we have supported her team, with Kimberly as coach, for "Odyssey of the Mind," an extracurricular creativity program. She also plays the trumpet, as did Bruce and his mother before him, in a 225-piece marching band at school, enjoying the full-regalia performances.

> Bruce relates:
> *Late one afternoon, I was standing in line with many other parents in a school cafeteria during registration season. One mother and her daughter, probably about 10 years old, were behind me. As they discussed which instrument the daughter would play when she enrolled in band class, the daughter pleaded, "Mom, I've always wanted to play the trombone. Can I play it?" Her mother responded, "Oh, honey, you don't want to play the trombone. Play a nice instrument like the flute." The daughter pleaded, "PLEASE let me play the trombone, PLEASE!!!" The mother answered, "No, you need to play a nice instrument," and this continued for several minutes.*

12. Take time for fun. In the busy pace of modern life, it's often easy to overlook this important aspect for building love and positive family relationships. An hour of positive interaction is worth more than several days of conflict. Family fun and time together holds families together. Recently, our family purchased over thirteen acres of land near our current home. The camping, fishing, gardening, nature watching, and exercising possibilities are endless. We plan to let the kids help choose and create the family fun. Family fun can be mutually planned and carried out every week, perhaps following a weekly family meeting.

Six

Empowering Children Through Reflective Listening

Negative Communication

Healthy communication is to family relationships what breathing is to life. Yet how many parent-child relationships wither and die because of destructive communication or no communication at all? While working toward her graduate degree, Kimberly learned that almost 90 percent of what parents say to children is negative—"Don't run out in the street," or "Why can't you come in on time?" Even affirmative communication such as "Do your homework" or "You can do better than that" has a negative connotation by implying that the child is not accomplishing something. Is it any wonder many children, particularly adolescents, tune out their parents after many years of negative messages? It's a form of emotional divorce from the parents. In many cases, the children are only trying to salvage their self-esteem. As discussed in the chapter "Encouraging Children," constructive criticism destroys parent-child communication by creating in children what is known as parent deafness.

Constant nagging, threatening, reminding, advising and ridiculing put a strain on relationships and create distance.

Communicating With Respect: The "I" Statement

When communicating about something that upsets you as a parent, an effective tool called "I" statements can keep the lines of communication and emotional doors open. "I" statements simply convey your feelings and the reasons for them, plus action to be taken. For example, "I'm concerned that if we don't get going, we'll be late for Grandma's party." As adults, if we're visiting with a friend but running late for an appointment, we might say politely, "I'm afraid I'll miss my appointment if I don't leave now, so we'll need to talk later." Instead, with our children, we often resort to threats or nagging to get the same response: "I've told you a hundred times—HURRY UP!" or "Get in the car right now or no friends over tomorrow." Treating children with the same respect we would treat a friend helps children feel valued, solicits their cooperation, and increases the likelihood of future responsibility.

Why do we sometimes talk with our children differently than we talk with a friend? Perhaps the reason we do is that our children are a captive audience with no choice in the matter, and our lives are too busy to worry much about their preferences. Parents and mental health professionals alike are often puzzled about the reasons children tend to rebel as teenagers. Could it be that they are finally old enough and big enough to demonstrate their anger and hostility toward the nagging, critical parent? Would your friends desire your companionship if you spoke to them like you speak to your child? We often feel as if children need to be spoken to in this way for effective discipline, forgetting the difference between correction and tearing down a self-image. We feel that when they get older, we'll treat them differently, but the die cannot be easily recast. Aggressive patterns can be set very early. Recent research in a university's family studies department found that power-assertive parenting—meaning parents use physical or verbal force to get their way with their children—tends to cause more aggressive and antisocial types of behavior in their own children.

Responses That Block Communication

To examine how to best communicate with children, imagine your-self and your child in the following situation and see whether you have played any of these roles. Also, try to put yourself in the child's place and think about how you would feel toward the parent who takes on these various roles.

Situation: After a two-family barbecue party hosted by another cou-ple, you return home with your child, who is in a terrible mood. Your child yells, "I'm never going over to Jeffrey's house again!" How do you react? What role do you play?

- *The Autocratic Parent* might set the child straight: "They are our friends, and as long as you live in this house with our rules, you will go over with us when we tell you to."

- *The Perfect Parent* who is overly concerned with family image would tell the child what he should do: "You know that's no way to talk—they are wonderful people and you should be grateful you have a friend. You should go back over there and make up right away."

- *The I-Know-Everything Parent* would placate the child in an attempt to showcase the parent's superior reasoning powers: "Now, now, you can't decide right now. You don't know enough about these things. Give it some time and you'll see that the best thing to do would be to . . . "

- *The Parent Judge* would pronounce the child guilty without a trial: "Oh, come on now—what did you do to Jeffrey this time?"

- *The Critical Parent* tears at the child's self-image: "You dumb kid—you don't know how to make friends. How come you think you're better than anyone, anyway?"

- *The Parent Psychiatrist* might attempt to diagnose and probe, and then guide the child to an outcome that is acceptable to the parent: "Now tell me all about the problem. Hmmm ... don't you feel that making up would be the best thing to do?"

- *The Overly Anxious Parent* excuses herself from dealing with the child because the parent feels she has too many worries as it is. This parent gives a patronizing pat on the back or the simplistic reassurance that things will work out—even if they won't: "Don't worry, you'll feel better in the morning. It'll all turn out fine."

Most parents assume these roles with the best of intentions. They know no other way of communicating and are probably replicating similar styles they learned and observed in their own families. Can you recall similar conversations in your home? You might not have felt understood, or worse, even felt unloved when you heard these closed-end, sometimes harsh responses.

All the above responses cut off further communication from children. These responses demonstrate to the child that the parent is unwilling to accept or understand what the child is trying to say. We wonder why teenagers choose peers over parents to disclose their thoughts and emotions. The reason is simple: Their friends don't lecture, reprimand, order, question, or judge. They listen. Most children, at least before their parent-child relationship is damaged, believe that their parents love them more than their friends do. So why do children reject their parents? The answer lies in the lack of communication training parents receive.

Bruce relates:

In my work with youth groups in church or sports, I'm amazed at how well kids communicate despite what we, their parents, would call their noncommunication of grunts, giggles, and secret code. The one thing I've noticed, from which parents could take a lesson, is their tendency to use

more open responses than adults do. Think about it. When
you were a teenager and you talked to your friends about
your parents' lack of understanding, they usually responded
empathetically with something like a classic 70's "Bummer,
man," or "I'd hate that too!" No lectures—friends just
listened.

A New Tool: FAB—*Feeling About Because*

Open responses, often called feeling reflection, allow children to feel accepted. The parent listener indicates that he understands or is attempting to understand the child's feelings. It is vital to convey your sincere wish and intention to understand. If you merely repeat your child's words back to him or her, parroting them insincerely, the child will not feel understood. Nonverbal cues, such as the look on your face and the tone of your voice, are vital in the process. A simple way of remembering this important communication skill is with three letters—FAB: *F*eeling *A*bout *B*ecause. Restate the *feeling* you think your child is expressing, add what situation you think the child is feeling *about*, and then the *because*, or the reason that he is feeling that way. In the above situation in which your child refuses to go back to Jeffrey's house, FAB would be used as follows: "I'm wondering if you *felt* disappointed *about* our visit with Jeffrey's family *because* he hurt you in some way."

Ideally, your child will give you enough information at the onset of your conversation to ascertain the feeling the child has and why, however, we often get only nonverbal cues. Since studies have shown that between 80 and 90 percent of all communication is nonverbal, you can train yourself to look for the smallest of cues to deduce a child's feelings. From the tapping of a foot, you can detect anxiety; tears usually mean sadness in younger children; clenched fists mean anger, and so on. Even if you guess the emotion, children will often correct you with a sense of relief if they believe you are genuinely trying to understand them.

Bruce relates:

I regularly ask graduate students in my international negotiations class to think about how the best negotiators in the world negotiate. Too often, we think of good negotiators as steely pit bulls who state their position and don't yield an inch. Although there is a place for win-lose bargaining and best-offer-first, good negotiation is more typically characterized by exploring options, mutual understanding, and creativity in expanding the pie. Superior negotiators restate the other party's position and summarize progress made to date. These are forms of FAB messages.

When getting started with your child, initially reflect on the feeling you think your child wants to convey. Give the feeling a name: "You sound *worried*." You can give the entire FAB message later when more information unfolds. Reflecting your child's feelings will not only improve communication by helping your child feel understood but also help the child work through difficulties. Children will understand their own emotions and learn to label them. They will be able to work through problems with peers and progress to the next important step: problem solving, which even most adults have difficulty doing. FAB responses act as a faucet by allowing children's feelings and ideas to flow unrestrained instead of constricting or even cutting off the flow with closed-end responses.

As parents volunteering in our school-aged children's classrooms and as therapists observing in clients' classrooms, we see many emotionally repressed children acting out their emotions through undesirable behavior. With untrained or unavailable parents, these children at school play out their emotions not expressed at home. They display their anger and frustrations with fists instead of words. Often the schools refer these children to a counselor who really does listen to them. For the first time, in many cases, the children's feelings are acknowledged and reflected. The children receive needed attention, redirect anger in more appropriate ways, and outwardly show improvement—at least until the child returns home. How much better it would be for a child's parents to understand and reflect the child's feelings and then help solve his problems on a day-to-day basis.

We recall our oldest daughter, who was eight years old at the time, storming in from playing outside one day yelling, "You're the meanest mom in the whole world!" Kimberly was tempted to retort with the perfect-parent response, "How could you talk like that—I've done nothing to hurt you!" With that, our daughter would have probably stomped to her room and slammed the door. Instead, Kimberly dealt with our daughter's anger by answering, "You're really angry with me it seems," the *feeling* part of the FAB message. Our daughter then went on, "I am angry because you won't let me have sleepovers on weeknights like Susie's mom lets her!" Kimberly was right—it was anger. Now what next? *About*, what and *Because*, the reason. Kimberly answered, "You feel angry that I won't let you have sleepovers on weeknights because you feel our family's rule is unfair?" They then had a meaningful discussion on getting enough rest and sleepovers and the reason that the two don't really go together. After sufficient venting of our daughter's emotion, Kimberly expressed her concern by using an "I" statement in the same FAB formula. "I'm puzzled about why we need to have sleepovers on weeknights, because we agreed that not one of us gets sleep." Mother and daughter then brainstormed, our daughter offering the first idea, about other times for sleepovers when she didn't need to get up early the next morning for school. After negotiation, they decided on weekends only for sleepovers.

This time it was easy. When things don't go as smoothly as in the example, we often defer family law discussions/changes to the next weekly family meeting. If Kimberly had not first reflected our daughter's feeling of anger, she would not have felt understood—she also would not have reached the more important brainstorming and decision-making stages.

Five Steps of Problem-Solving Communication

To summarize, the process of effective and responsible problem solving with children includes the following steps.

1. *Reflect the child's feelings* using the FAB formula. If the emotion is strong, severely repressed, or nonverbal, you may need to respond with several feeling-reflective sentences before the child is willing or able to start brainstorming and trying to solve the problem.

2. *Explore all alternatives* available to the child. Let the child suggest alternatives and give encouragement if she appears hesitant; for example, "Keep thinking—I know you'll come up with something!" If you jump in with your perfect ideas, your child will be hampered in developing her own. First, suggesting your course of action tends to stifle creativity, and the action you recommend may not actually be the best alternative, certainly not one that the child will feel is her own to implement. Even more damaging to the relationship, the child may blame you if your suggestion proves to be the wrong thing to do.

3. *Discuss probable outcomes* of each alternative explored. "What might happen if you choose that?" Without judging, guide your child in a healthy discussion of each likely result of the different plans of action he chooses. Take time to discuss each probable scenario that could play out in your child's life.

4. *Choose an alternative.* Have your child commit to one alternative that he feels best solves the problem. Making a decision and sticking with it, even if it may not be the perfect solution, is a valuable skill children can learn at an early age. Be careful not to second-guess or discourage the child's decision unless the consequences are grave and have not been fully explored or comprehended by the child.

5. *Plan time for evaluation.* Discuss when you will follow up on the decision and the outcome. When that time comes, evaluate what happened and why and what, if anything, the child would choose to do differently in the future.

Children must walk before they can run, master algebra and trigonometry before they can take on calculus. Yet we often rob them of the chance to learn the skill of making small decisions, which will teach them how to make the more important decisions later in life, such as a career choice, or a partner to marry. The decision-making process creates responsible, creative, and emotionally healthy children who communicate well using reflective listening. The process also bonds parents to their children without developing overly dependent children with overly protective parents.

An Example of Dealing With a Tyrannical Teacher

This same daughter previously mentioned entered kindergarten when she was four years and ten months old. We used the FAB process we outlined above to discover she was in crisis after the second day of school. The symptom of the problem was that she would not sleep in her own bed. Without using reflective listening and problem solving, we might have concluded that her sleep problem resulted from immature or stubborn behavior or that it was just a stage she was going through, given the newness of kindergarten. After this behavior continued for two nights, Kimberly asked, "Are you scared to sleep in your own bed?" She affirmed with a nod. Kimberly then reflected again, "You're scared to sleep in your bed and you'd rather sleep on the family room couch?" Our daughter then went on to describe her fears, which led to a play-by-play account of the second day of school when a craft was being taught. The teacher asked the children to color, then cut the design. Our daughter either didn't hear or chose not to do the craft in that order. Instead, she cut the design first and then colored it. In response, the teacher tore up her design in front of the class, made her put her head down on her desk, took away her class job, and stamped her papers with sad faces for the remainder of the day. This was the second day of kindergarten! The story shocked us so that we asked the teacher whether it was true. The teacher confirmed that it was. She chose this course of action, she said, because she must be hard on the children the first week to show them who is boss—"kind of like breaking horses," the teacher said.

We refrained from marching into the principal's office and forming a figurative lynching party for the teacher, which was our first reaction. Instead, we went home to deal with the problem with our daughter. We again reflected her feelings on the matter, helped her explore alternatives, and talked through the consequences of each plan. Our daughter decided that she was so fearful of the teacher she wanted to change to another class. She asked if we could speak to the "nice principal" for her, and we did. We merely told him that we felt our daughter needed a different learning environment, given the events of the week and hoped that he could assist us. He granted our request to transfer her, but added in the teacher's defense that the children must obey in the classroom. We well understood that order, not chaos, should prevail in a classroom, but our daughter's actions hardly qualified as provoking an uprising. If children obey only out of fear, their self-esteem and relationships with authority figures suffer. We noticed in our subsequent volunteer visits to the school that more than an average number of children in that kindergarten class were excessively aggressive on the playground. We shudder to think of what our daughter's kindergarten year could have been had we not really listened to what she was feeling and helped her solve the problem. Our daughter was placed with a nurturing teacher who provided the environment necessary for her developmental growth and a more positive first-time school experience.

Kimberly relates:

Janice's parents failed to truly listen to her. Janice, 13 years old, was brought to treatment because she refused to go to school and had frequent nightmares of her parents and other beloved relatives dying. Thus far, her parents had dealt with the problem by forcing her to go to school, stating that it's a law and she had to go. Her parents had not yet questioned Janice about her dreams or her reasons for suddenly refusing to go to school. In our first session, I used cards that have the names of feelings on them and asked Janice to pinpoint the emotions surrounding her school refusal. She chose the frightened card and told me that the previous week, a sixth-grade bully accosted her on the playground and had threatened to kill her. As I probed deeper, with reflective listening, I also learned that her parents had recently separated, which made her severely anxious and deeply threatened her security. Her anxiety was surfacing in the form of nightmares, transferring to school and to the school bully as well. After brainstorming about the bully, she chose to confront him at school with an "I feel, I want" statement (an abbreviated FAB). She decided to say, "It makes me angry when you threaten me at school, and I want you to stop." If he continued to bully her, she would next say, "If you keep doing this, I will tell the principal—you choose!" After confronting the bully directly, he found other less assertive children to harass. With the bully problem under control, her fears now surfaced in the form of increased anxiety due to the unsettling family difficulties at home. I told her parents to encourage Janice to attend school and reflect her anxieties as they surfaced. Janice disclosed that her parents would often fight and never spend time together alone. I chose to deal with that family problem by encouraging her parents to have date nights together. Janice was so excited about the possibility of her parents spending time together that she worked out a plan to make this possible by offering to baby-sit her six-year-old sister. After spending much needed time together, her parents began to take more interest in each other and also in their children's emotional health. Janice's nightmares, anxieties, and school fears disappeared.

Janice learned how to deal with her own anxieties because someone listened. It is important for parents to resist the urge to impose their solutions before allowing the child to find ways of solving the problems. Often, children can solve their own problems by merely talking to a sympathetic adult who can offer guidance on the advantages and disadvantages of various courses of action. More about the challenges of problem solving, both within and outside home, is discussed in the next chapter, "Problem Ownership and Resolution."

Seven

Problem Ownership and Resolution

T he Protective but Permissive Parent

Ironically, one of life's greatest disadvantages for a child can be an overinvolved parent. The problem can start with the best of intentions, wishing to spare the child the pain of failure or the embarrassment of a job not as well done as another child's. Nevertheless, such parents can eventually do everything for their children, often becoming their children's servants. The children, knowing no differently, begin to exploit their parents' kindness, which ends up in too much leniency or permissiveness from the parents. Thus, overcontrol and permissiveness can actually become different sides of the same problem. The parents take responsibility for everything the children do, believing that their children's behavior reflects on their competence as parents and their worth as people. Parents can be so concerned with their image in the neighborhood and community that they control their child's every move, robbing the child of independence necessary for healthy emotional development. Instead of respecting the children by letting them learn from their own experiences, these parents overprotect their youngsters from all consequences in life, preventing the children from learning on their own. For many of these parents, keeping their children dependent on them gives them purpose or a sense of importance. These well-intentioned parents remind and coax constantly with such statements as, "Let me see your homework," "Polish your shoes," "Change your clothes," not giving the child a chance to assume responsibility.

There is a difference between doing things for children and doing things with them. We are not suggesting that you spend less time with your children. We are suggesting that your time with your children should not be spent doing things for them that they can and should do for themselves. Also, don't try to force them to do something your way, especially if that something concerns them, and not you. Because society holds many unrealistic expectations for parents and children to excel in everything they do, parents tend to overprotect and control. Only when parents decide that responsibility instilled in their children is more important than the opinion of others will their children begin to develop self-esteem, confidence, and responsibility.

Setting Limits

Most children need and actually want their parents to set reasonable boundaries.

Kimberly relates:

I recall working with a teen who had been arrested and taken to jail twice for shoplifting. Each time, his father—a policeman—and his mother bailed him out of jail immediately to avoid their own embarrassment. He did not learn the consequences for stealing because his parents were too concerned with their own images. Subconsciously, the teen used this fact to his own manipulative advantage. He was seeking revenge against his parents for what he perceived autocratic control of his rights regarding his friends, his phone calls, and his clothing. His methods of retaliation were ultimately hurting him. His track coach found out about his stealing and removed him from the team.

> *Children, like this teen, eventually become increasingly dis-*
> *couraged if limits are not set. Permissive parents feel they are*
> *protecting their children, without realizing they are handi-*
> *capping them. The teen's stealing could have been stopped*
> *with one night in jail, but instead had become a habit when*
> *he was finally brought to my office for treatment. The prob-*
> *lem was parents too permissive to set limits and too control-*
> *ling to let him suffer the consequences of his own actions.*

Many families in Kimberly's practice have children who abuse alcohol and drugs because limits have not been set by their parents. In losing respect for themselves, these children continue down the path of self-destruction. Through appropriate communication and limit setting, children can learn to deal with discouragement in ways other than substance abuse or other destructive behavior.

When parents control and dominate, they violate respect for their child. In a different manifestation of the same problem, when parents become permissive doormats, they violate respect for them-selves. Also, parents who overdo for children capable of doing for themselves or parents who give in to their children at their own expense teach children that parents' rights are not to be highly val-ued. In either situation, parents are failing to teach children the con-cept of mutual respect. Parents need to be firm about their own rights without being domineering or depriving the child of her rights.

A mother we know was talking on the phone when her son entered the room and turned the volume up on the radio. The moth-er stated her feelings and rights calmly with an "I" statement: "I'm frustrated because I can't hear when the radio is loud; please either turn it down or listen to your radio in another room." This estab-lished the mother's rights while allowing her son to choose his course of action to solve the problem.

When our children forget their school lunches, we do not hop quickly in the car and take them the lunch, even when they call from school. They might try to make us feel responsible for their lunch, but we refrain from feeling guilty. Taking lunch to them would not help them remember to take lunch the next day, nor would it help them become more responsible in the future. We are not suggesting that all forgetfulness be treated in this manner. Sometimes, forgetting can be fatal ("Sorry, son, you forgot to take your insulin"). A parent needs to discern the appropriate age and situation that requires a child to be responsible. A healthy child will not starve to death by missing lunch one day, but will probably not make the same mistake again when he realizes who is responsible for taking the lunch. Since lunch is each child's responsibility, going hungry is his problem.

> Kimberly relates:
>
> *In working with families over the past fifteen years, I have occasionally seen extremely manipulative children who threaten to call the authorities to report child neglect if the parents don't bring their forgotten lunch. They insist it is still the parents' responsibility to make and deliver all meals, even if the child forgot to take lunch to school. My response to democratic parents is to have their child call the family pediatrician before making any false accusation that could remove the child from the comfort of home. The pediatricians I have worked with throughout the years feel that a missed meal due to irresponsibility can teach a child an important lesson in life, barring any diagnosed illness that requires constant and consistent food intake—diabetes, for example.*

In our family, when a situation is a child's problem, we reflect feelings with an FAB message and help brainstorm for a solution to *their* problem. After reflecting our daughter's sadness about forgetting her lunch, we explored options available to her. Ultimately, she chose to borrow money from a friend who had offered her a loan. She didn't tell us that originally. She had said, "Oh, I'll just call my parents," hoping we would solve her problem for her. She became a more responsible girl that day because we refrained from taking responsibility for her problem.

Whose Problem Is This, Really?

When a problem arises between you and your child, ask yourself the question, "Is this my problem, or is it hers?" A rule of thumb to use is that the person who gets upset about the problem is usually the person who owns it, whether she should or not. Parents often become upset about situations that should concern only their children. Parents who act on problems that children consciously or subconsciously feel are theirs foster at the very least irresponsibility and at the worst rebellion in their children. No one likes to have someone else interfere in decisions that affect him alone.

Here's a pop quiz. Test yourself to see how well you understand the issue of problem ownership. On the line opposite each, write P if you feel the problem is the parents' responsibility or write C if you think the child is responsible. Ask yourself, Whose reasonable rights are *not* being met? That is the key to who owns the problem.

The Problem	*Who Owns It*
1. Difficulty with peers	_____
2. Conflict with teachers	_____
3. Failure to clean up home common areas	_____
4. Poor grades at school	_____
5. Misbehavior at the dinner table	_____
6. Conflict with siblings	_____

How did you do? Of course, your opinion may differ from ours, but we would say that only problems three and five are problems owned by the parents. These two problems impose on the rights of the parents and therefore come under the responsibility of the parents. Problems such as these should be handled assertively by the parents to ensure their reasonable rights and to meet their needs. "I" statements are initially effective when dealing with a problem that you own.

Parent-Owned Problems

In problem three, failure to clean up home common areas, the parent could say, "I feel uncomfortable in our home when messes are left—I need them cleaned up." This does two things: It vents emotion and resentment in a reasonable way and lets the offending children know the feelings and expectations of the parent. In this instance, permissive parents would continue to clean up messes for their children, believing that the children are less capable or alternatively more important than themselves. Resentment builds, blowups occur, and the parents impose martial law when they finally get fed up with the irresponsibility. Autocratic parents would initially lecture, command, judge, and preach and then wonder that their children tune them out. Threats and punishment don't teach children responsibility—they teach manipulation of the system to avoid getting caught.

Problem five, misbehavior at the dinner table, poses a unique challenge for parents. Often, expressing feelings and expectations takes care of potential problems. Simply state the expectation in a firm but friendly, nonjudgmental tone, "I'm concerned about the milk spill on the table, and I need you to take care of it, please." The consequence of meal interruption and cleanup discourages repeated behavior. This "I" statement doesn't blame the child but encourages him by showing that you trust the child to behave responsibly and show respect for all concerned. To handle the problem, a permissive parent might clean up the mess for the child, assuming that all children go through a sloppy stage or that cleaning up is just what parents do. Accidents will continue to occur and responsibility and respect are never fostered.

An "I" statement, however, becomes a threat and sounds autocratic if expressed by parents angrily. Parents should remember how they communicate their feelings to friends, using nonverbal messages like tone of voice, posture, and eye contact. As discussed previously, if parents talked to their friends as they do to their children, would their friends still remain their friends? Some parents expect their children to be courteous and respectful to them, and yet they criticize, lecture, punish, and distrust their children.

If the parent owns the problem and has expressed feelings and expectations appropriately but the child still does not respond, the next step is to employ a natural or logical consequence that has been discussed beforehand with the child. We all know what happens if we are caught speeding, yet we do it because we believe the chance of getting caught is unlikely. When rights are violated and "I" statements are ignored, implementing creative, consistent consequences engenders responsibility and respect. (To structure these consequences, see the chapters "Consequences that Create Responsibility" and "Consequences for Specific Challenges.")

The autocratic parent yells, belittles, and threatens the child. The child obeys from fear, or rebels, maintaining that "nobody can treat me that way." This child, especially a teenager, finds other ways of hurting an autocratic parent. When the problem is the child's, the parent should reflect the child's feelings and explore alternatives to help the child solve the problem. Attempting to solve children's problems for them makes them dependent, irresponsible, and angry, especially if the parent's solution fails.

Child-Owned Problems

Problem one on page ooo, difficulty with peers, can present perhaps a real challenge for children. When dealing with the school bully, kids who are ill equipped usually do nothing. They either repress their emotions or try unsuccessfully to stand up to the bully. Typically, children are bullies because they have low self-esteem and receive little or no attention at home. Many are abused and seek to abuse others to make themselves feel better. Taking an active approach empowers children to refuse becoming the victims. Child victims become adult victims if they do not learn to stand up for themselves.

Handling Bullying and Teasing

In the chapter "Empowering Children Through Reflective Listening," Janice used an "I feel, I want" statement to release her emotions and attempt to stop the threats of the bully on the playground. Often, this active stance will stop the victimization. When it does not, children can continue their active position by stating the consequence that will occur if the behavior continues. For Janice, that meant that she would tell the principal if it continued. No child likes to be a "tattletale," but sometimes telling a teacher or principal stops the problem. Notice that Janice was not going to tell the principal unless the bully chose that consequence. A simple, "You made the choice for me to tell the principal. I asked you to stop and I told you what would happen if you didn't," did the trick. This active approach tells the bully, "I won't be bullied."

With teasing, the fogging technique works wonders. Without agreeing to the teasing, the child assertively throws up a smokescreen by giving deflective answers without becoming defensive, which would only validate the attack. If a teaser makes insulting, untrue accusations, responses such as "maybe so", "could be", or "that's possible" work effectively. These responses discourage the aggressor by showing that the child refuses to be affected by put-downs. Generally, the person teasing does not stop after only one attempt. The child should continue to use fogging until the assaults stop. If the teasing person states the obvious truth, like "You're tardy—you'll get in trouble!" the child could respond with "Yup, I sure am late!" which doesn't give the teaser ammunition to further the conflict.
Example:

> *Teaser:* "You can't play baseball."
> *Child:* "So I can't. So what?"
> *Teaser:* "Everyone will laugh at you."
> *Child:* "Maybe."
> *Teaser:* "No one will pick you for their team."
> *Child:* "Maybe."
> *Teaser:* "Everyone will stare at you and call you names."
> *Child:* "Maybe so."

By not fighting back, the child diffuses or fogs the assaults. The teaser then loses interest in teasing a child that refuses to be annoyed.

The fogging technique can prevent further assaults, thus protecting the child's self-esteem.

Preventing Meltdown of Standards

Alcohol, drugs, sex, gangs, cheating, stealing—the list of parent nightmares goes on and on. When your child is confronted by a peer who wants your child to compromise the standards you have painstakingly tried to instill, the broken record approach can be very effective. Like a deep scratch on a record that plays a segment over and over, the child's responses wear down the "friend," who eventually gives up. The classmate who wants your child to cheat on tests could be answered with, "You're a good friend, but I don't share answers." When confronted again, the same answer is given and continues to be given until the confronter stops the requests. The broken record is composed of a kind statement plus the child's policy on the issue ("I like you, but I won't ..."). Stated in a matter-of-fact tone, the perpetrator gets the message that there are no exceptions. When dealing with a drug pusher or "let's have a drink" buddy, the broken record approach works. "I never use drugs" or "I don't drink." No matter how many times the child is asked, the same answer is given. Perhaps the child, realizing that the friend is really no friend at all, will end the relationship with no nagging from you.

Kimberly relates:

A 12-year-old client whose family has a history of being victimized by lack of assertiveness described how she was enticed to smoke by a friend. Initially, the client declined by saying, "No, thanks, you can though." Her friend continued to manipulate and push her, hoping by lowering my client's standards, the friend would feel better about her own low status. After three requests, my client thought she should smoke to please her friend, without realizing that she was compromising her own good sense. She then lost self-esteem, and it took several sessions to practice a more assertive stance to protect her values. We used the broken record approach initially and then used an "I feel, I want" statement: "I feel frustrated that I have to keep telling you that I don't smoke, and I wish you would stop asking." If the friend continued pushing, the consequence should also be stated: "If you choose to keep pressuring me, I will leave and break off our friendship." After many attempts to bolster her assertiveness by using the broken record response, the client successfully turned down cigarettes from this friend, with whom she soon chose to part company.

Peer pressure is a significant influence today, making it increasingly difficult to go against the crowd, even if that crowd is only one other person. When parents reflect a child's disappointment with friends who don't share or support his or her standards, the child will often realize how little those persons mean to him or her. In time, without being forced, children will see these peers for what they really are and ultimately choose not to associate with them. Attempting to force children away from the wrong crowd, as many parents of teens will attest, can backfire, resulting in rebellion.

A large group of teachers Kimberly had addressed in a local school district recently gathered to discuss a growing problem in this country: violence in the classroom. One teacher related an experience of a student who had pulled out a knife during class. The teacher had panicked, feeling out of control. Even in this instance, where a quick, cool-headed response was needed, an "I feel, I want" approach with a choice can be very effective. "I'm worried for the safety of the other students. I want you to hand the knife to me or I will come and get it from you—which will it be?" If the child continues to refuse, the teacher can then state a tougher consequence: "If you don't hand it over, I'll have the police here in a few minutes and you'll be taken to jail." Anyone brandishing a knife is out of control. By remaining in control, the situation can be handled. With metal detectors installed at many schools, this problem has become a reality with which many teachers must now deal.

Kimberly relates:

Recently I was working with a teenager who was attending a local high school. He had been threatened with a gun by another student because my client had "looked at his girlfriend" from across campus. The incident was reported immediately to school authorities, and the violent student was removed from school, but continued to harass the teen, including issuing death threats. Because the gun-wielding student knew where the teenager lived, the threatened boy's family was so concerned that they moved from the area to a new school district, at their son's suggestion. Supporting this young man and allowing him to make his own decision really empowered my client and he was able to adapt to his new setting very quickly.

The Tyrannical Teacher, Part 2

Problem two, conflict with teachers, poses dilemmas for many teens. The example discussed previously of our daughter's problem with her kindergarten teacher was quite easily solved. The situation for older children is more complex. As soon as feasible, older children should handle most conflicts with teachers on their own, unless gross negligence by a teacher is obvious. Parents who jump in to solve their children's problems with teachers can have the opposite effect. First, the parents take away the responsibility of school experience that rightly belongs to the student. Second, the insertion of another party into the conflict may only serve to heighten misunderstandings. Third, and most important, parents can rob their child of problem-solving skills needed to cope in an increasingly complex, unfair world. Teachers and bosses are only a few of the people that children will need to deal with in life. FAB statements and "I feel, I want" sentences can be constructed and used very effectively with a teacher. We have had success in encouraging our own children to deal directly with their teachers to solve problems of all kinds—from seating assignments to accusations of breaking school rules.

Kimberly relates:

A high school teenager with whom I worked recently encountered a difficult situation with a teacher. Many students had attempted to transfer to another teacher's class, but to no avail. My client felt she had been given an unfair grade and chose to approach the teacher after school using an "I feel, I want" strategy. She said, "I feel that a D grade is unfair, based on my test scores and homework, and I would like you to reevaluate my scores, please." With responsible teachers, this approach generally works, but not with this teacher, who refused the request. During our next session, the student brainstormed another approach, adding a consequence as well: "I have requested a reevaluation of my grade because I feel that it was unfair. If you choose to turn down my request, I will need to approach school administration with my problem." The results were a higher grade and increased respect for the student. Had she not set limits with this teacher nor dealt assertively with the problem, she would still have a D grade and would have compromised her self-esteem.

Poor Grades

Problem four, poor grades, as in the example above, are the child's problem. Many parents attempt to take this problem on themselves for undoubtedly noble motives—helping the child succeed later in life. But if parents become overly involved, the child's school performance can worsen. All parents want to see their children succeed and do well, but forcing them to perform can result in irresponsibility and can cause rebellion.

By setting a good example, parents can help young children develop responsible habits. Work before play sets the homework standard in a family. We should not nag children about their homework unless teachers report at conference that the children are not trying their best. If so, children should restructure their time and priorities to devote more energy to school work. They should not do what they *want* to do until they complete what *needs* doing. Parents' jobs are to work and maintain the home. Children's responsibilities are school and chores. Children should not be allowed to take on extracurricular activities unless their grades represent their best efforts.

> Bruce relates:
> *I help coach my son's basketball team. After we noticed a slip our in son's graded assignments, I handed him the front page of the Saturday morning newspaper's sports section. The headline read "[Star Player] Suspended for Poor Grades." I made it clear that if he did not do his best in school, he would be sitting on the bench as well. I explained the concept of academic probation and said, "If it's good enough for NCAA athletes, it's good enough for you." Not that we expect him to get straight As, but we do expect him to study and do well on tests that require effort. For example, spelling should be one of the easiest subjects, not the hardest—a child only needs to put forth an effort to memorize the words. After sitting out a game because of lack of effort, he quickly figured it out. I talked with the head coach, who was very supportive. The coach said that too many parents blame coaches for a child's poor attitude—of course they want to see their kid play—instead of using athletics as a tool to train their child.*

The policies of most schools now reflect the value of academics first. High GPAs must be maintained for many sports programs and other extracurricular activities. Much media attention went to the recent NBA player lockout—owners not letting their teams practice—over salaries. One high school coach locked out his own team—not over money, but over grades. His student-athletes were not keeping their academic commitments. The only practice was held in the library for a few weeks. We applaud that coach. Even car insurance companies will give better rates to students with higher grades.

The local video store in our town gives a free movie rental to any student who can produce at least a B report card at the checkout counter. With no intervention, children can learn to be responsible for their own school performance.

When children do not perform to their best abilities in school, there are three general reasons:

- Laziness
- Power struggle
- Discouragement and feelings of inadequacy

When children believe that grades are their responsibility and not the responsibility of their parents, they will usually work to improve them. Children of parents in academia are notorious for underachieving to get back at parents who try to force good grades, which reflects a power struggle.

If a child becomes discouraged about grades, reflect his or her feelings with an FAB message. Because grades are the child's problem, you can help explore alternatives to improve the grades. Privileges and opportunities should be minimal when children are not achieving at *their* best level. As discussed in the last chapter, wait before giving advice. First, try to exhaust all the child's ideas on improving the situation. Children usually know what they should do and only need encouragement from parents. Plan a time for evaluation after obtaining a commitment, and then reevaluate the program if necessary.

Kimberly relates:
Sally informed me, before telling her parents, that she was getting D grades in three classes. Since this was the first time she had brought home such low grades, Sally felt embarrassed and didn't want to tell her parents. She had been lazy about doing her homework and studying for tests and was now facing the harsh consequence of not prioritizing well. We brainstormed together and came up with an afternoon schedule that mandated homework before friends.

Also, she chose to go in early twice a week to get extra help from the math teacher. She needed to catch up in those areas in which she was far behind. She made a commitment to study for tests. We discussed the possibility of her needing to repeat the D classes to raise her GPA. She was motivated.

Luckily, her parents supported her efforts and could see she needed to learn from her own experience. In their parent-child agreement, baby-sitting for others and excessive activities were curtailed until homework was completed and grades improved. Unfortunately, many parents only use the stick approach and punish for bad grades. As a result, the student loses motivation and grades actually go down, because the student thinks, "I'll show you who is in charge!"

Sibling Rivalry

Problem six, conflict with siblings, has posed an interesting problem for parents for many generations. It would be less of a problem if parents recognized it as a problem between the children themselves. As discussed in the chapter "Why Children Misbehave," behavior always serves a purpose. Children attempt to involve parents to gain their attention or to have the parents find the solutions for them. Often children seek revenge by exerting power over the perceived favorite of the parents, which leads to fights among siblings. Many parents excuse the fighting as normal and only a stage children go through. Although fighting is common, it is not necessarily normal and need not be accepted.

Often children observe parents fighting and conclude that fighting must be an acceptable way of resolving conflict. When parents don't fight between themselves and do not get involved in the disagreements of their children, the children will begin to assume ownership of their sibling disagreements. Parents should remove themselves when a conflict arises. Mom or Dad can go into another room, explaining, "The conflict is between you and your sister. I know you can resolve it together." If you observe your children unnoticed, you will see that they can resolve their own conflicts when left alone. Kimberly recalls as a child her mother, after attending a parenting course, telling her and her brother that she would no longer referee their fights. It was amazing how the bickering and tattling ceased.

After leaving the conflict, parents may notice the conflict follows them, another indication that the children are fighting for their parents to notice and to take ownership of the problem. Most children will not physically harm each other in a fight. If a child becomes out of control and picks up a dangerous object such as a stick or a rock, simply remove the object and inform the children to resolve their conflict in another way. Young children can be distracted from a conflict with older children by removing them from the scene. Often, younger children provoke their older siblings, and the older child shouldn't be blamed for becoming irritated. When appropriate and possible, older and younger children should be given a chance to work out their own relationships.

The only exceptions to children working out their own conflicts are fighting in a part of the house where a parent is bothered, fighting in a dangerous area, or fighting where damage to family property could result. Clearly, in these instances, the parent must actively set limits by first using an "I feel, I want" statement, such as "I worry when I see wrestling near the lamp, and I want you to go outside if you choose to continue."

To summarize:
When the child has the problem:
1.   Reflect the child's feelings, using a reflective listening response such as an FAB message (*Feeling About Because*).
2.   Explore alternatives with the child and allow the child to brainstorm and choose his or her own solution.

When the parent has the problem:
1.   State your feelings about your problem using "I feel, I want".
2.   Devise an appropriate limit, discussed in the chapter "Consequences That Create Responsibility," if stating your feeling wasn't enough.
3.   Plan a time, such as a family meeting, to reevaluate or revise the process.

Eight

Consequences that Create Responsibility

According to *American Demographics,* in 1997, 30 percent of all U.S. adults believed that most kids are lazy; half believed that many kids are spoiled. On the other hand, about 30 percent of teenagers believed that parents who don't know how to communicate with kids or parents who think that buying things for kids equate with caring for them were very common. Clearly, we have our work cut out for us as parents, and parents everywhere want to do a better job. From 1991 and 1995, the percentage of U.S. adults who agree that politeness and good manners are among the most important qualities that parents can instill in their children rose ten percentage points to 59 percent.

In previous chapters, we discussed the two most common but misguided parenting styles of parents with children today—autocracy and permissiveness. The *autocratic* parent forces, controls, punishes, and rewards to elicit the child's cooperation. The *permissive* parent uses some of the same techniques, yet ultimately gives in to the child, becoming a doormat. Both types of parenting attempt to teach responsibility, but both fail to do so. To learn responsibility, children need to be assigned responsibility for their actions and ultimately reap the benefits or suffer the consequences of the decisions they make.

The Ineffectiveness of Rewards and Punishment

Autocratic and permissive styles of discipline, with their subjective rewards and punishments, are how most parents of today were raised. These styles have several disadvantages.

1. Attempting to force children to conform rarely brings about the intended result.
2. Children learn to behave only when rewarded or in the presence of authority figures.
3. Rewards and punishments place the responsibility for a child's behavior with the parent, not the child, because the parent decides what is good and bad. This unintentionally encourages continued irresponsibility in children.
4. Children never develop self-discipline and live their lives in the reactive mode, thinking, "If I act this way, I'll get that." By not making their own decisions, they become increasingly dependent on rewards or the lack of punishment. This leads to insecurity, resentfulness, and rebellion.
5. Punishment focuses on past behaviors and dwells on the child's mistakes. Punishments are arbitrary and are not the natural or logical result of behaviors.

The Principle of Natural and Logical Consequences

The concept of allowing children to learn from their experiences is referred to as natural and logical consequences. Without coercion, control, or corporal punishment, parents prepare the child for the ways that nature and society will react to his behavior.

Perhaps the best way of introducing this concept is an example from our own family. When our oldest daughter was 6 years old, she ran across the street without looking both ways to play with a friend. We had reminded her constantly, but she chose not to pay attention to our warnings. Not too long before, a neighbor had been killed by a car, but the danger of running in the street had yet to sink in. On this particular occasion, we first expressed an "I feel, I want" statement: "We worry about your safety when you don't look both ways before crossing the busy street, and we need you to behave more responsibly." Bruce had witnessed the event and saw that the car missed her by just a few feet.

We brainstormed with her about how she could act more responsibly when crossing the street. She suggested that she should forfeit crossing the street to play with friends for a penalty of one day for every inch the car had missed her. Her father estimated that the car had missed her by about six feet, which would amount to a penalty of 72 days. We suggested that an appropriate consequence would be one day for every foot by which the car had missed her. After only three days of not crossing the street to play with friends, she was truly feeling the consequence of her irresponsible behavior. Because none of her friends lived on our side of the street, this was an appropriate, logical consequence. After the six days were served, she remembered to look both ways before crossing the street, without experiencing the natural result of injury to her body. Although we had discussed our feelings about street safety with our children before, a consequence had to be devised immediately to increase responsible behavior. No other method of child discipline would have changed her ways so permanently. A few months later, our 3-year-old attempted the same irresponsible behavior. After crossing without looking a second time, he chose to remain in the house for the remainder of the day.

Many well-meaning parents, who have not learned any different method of disciplining, would have spanked or yelled at their child to show her the pain that could accompany an accident if the behavior were to go unchecked. We believe, however, that physical punishment elicits more fear and anger instead of changing a pattern of behavior. The result is not increased cooperation or responsible behavior. For any consequence to be effective, the child must see it as logical—spanking or yelling are not. Children remember the spanking but not the behavior that provoked it. Corporal punishment engenders fear and creates dysfunction in family relationships. When teaching parenting classes, Kimberly often asks parents what they would do if their spouse or a friend spanked them when they did something to offend the spouse or friend. Short relationship! After the laughing subsides, she explains that it is no wonder children ultimately emotionally divorce abusive parents. This new discipline method requires parents to think logically rather than punitively, creating respect for both children and parents.

> Bruce relates:
>
> *My mother, the sweetest person I've ever known, introduced me to natural and logical consequences with quiet but amazing effectiveness when I was 16 years old. I worked on a paint crew at the University of Utah during high school summers. I was to be at work very early, 6:00 a.m. as I recall. After several mornings of dragging me out of bed, one morning she let me sleep in. I woke up late, of course, totally exasperated, to find my mother calmly reading the paper at the table. No words were exchanged—I knew what had happened. I arrived at work late—the supervisor had to make a special trip to drive me to the work site. I realized that it was my responsibility to get up in the morning, not my mother's.*

Effectiveness of Logical Consequences

Consequences work when even the youngest children can grasp the logic.

1. Logical consequences encourage respect for everyone and reflect the reality of the social and natural order of things, rather than the power or personal authority of the parent.
2. Consequences that are logical relate to the behavior.
3. Unlike punishment, logical consequences imply no judgment or condemnation of the child. The emphasis is on the deed not the doer.
4. Logical consequences encourage responsible behavior in the future whereas other punishments encourage further negative behavior.
5. Logical consequences focus on building relationships rather

than destroying them. When invoking consequences, speak in a friendly and matter-of-fact tone. Emphasize the child's choice as opposed to censure.

The purpose of natural and logical consequences is to motivate children to make more responsible decisions. Punishment forces submission and encourages dependency and possibly rebellion. By experiencing consequences each time the misbehavior occurs the child develops self-discipline and internal motivation.

One hundred percent consistency is the key. Random or inconsistent consequences are ineffective. If you consider why most Americans speed, you realize that it is the lack of negative consequences for disobeying the law. If you do happen to get caught, you may think twice about speeding during the months following. Your speed may drop temporarily, but without consistent consequences, you soon return to the old habit of speeding until the next ticket, if it ever comes.

As a therapist, Kimberly often asks parents to estimate the percentage of follow-through on consequences actually implemented with their children. Most feel satisfied with following through even 50 percent of the time. When Kimberly asks them if they would buy a lottery ticket with a guarantee of winning only 50 percent of the time, they understand their children's continuing misbehavior.

Consequences are only effective if parents do not have hidden motives, such as winning or controlling their children. Parents must be both firm and kind when using consequences. Firmness refers to parental follow-through, and kindness refers to the manner in which the choice is presented. Although firmness and kindness are not easy to implement in the same action, with practice, parents can learn the skill.

A popular Disney example of combining these two qualities can be found in the nanny Mary Poppins. She was very firm in safeguarding her own rights and the rights of others and in maintaining harmony in the home. She was kind and respectful but also a lot of fun. A recent newspaper article on our family actually compared Kimberly's style to that of Mary Poppins, which we took as a compliment.

Bruce relates:

In all of my course syllabi, I have included the phrase "late assignments, except in the most extraordinary of verifiable circumstances, will receive no credit." Natural and logical consequences also work for graduate business students, some of whom, incredible as it seems, have not learned how the world works. Two students came to my office last year with late assignments. The first was obviously sick as a dog, doctor's visit bill in hand, apologizing that her assignment was late. She received no penalty. The second had been too busy with other things to attend classes, worked at a small family business, and basically, forgot about the assignment. Though I commend his frankness, he had no verifiable, legitimate excuse. He received no credit. Amazingly, he didn't seem to care. I thought of the difference in the upbringing of the two students. The first must have been taught by natural and logical consequences on taking responsibility for her actions. The second, probably raised by well-meaning parents, was bailed out of trouble time and time again, failing to suffer consequences for his actions.

The Natural Order of Things

Without a doubt, the world we live in contains cynicism, oppressiveness, and irresponsibility—qualities parents do not want in their children. Regardless, the responsible elements of society—education, law enforcement, and concerned friends and neighbors—can actually assist parents in teaching responsibility to their children. The world around our children, in addition to the environment in our homes, can be the source of the natural and logical consequences that teach children responsibility. Without the parent's interference, the teenager who drinks and drives must face the judge and jail time. The child who does not play fairly with friends finds himself with no playmates; the child who neglects homework must answer to a teacher. We believe that schoolwork is a child's job until adulthood. Parents can help overburdened teachers by curtailing extracurricular activities and other opportunities if their child is not doing his or her best at the most important job of childhood.

> Bruce relates:
>
> *A variation of the "I didn't do my assignment" speech is the "please change my grade" plea, incredible coming from graduate students. Every semester, one or two students come in asking for a grade change after the final exam is graded and the grades posted. "I'll lose my scholarship," "I won't get a good job" are just two of the reasons given for improving their grade—reasons they should have thought of before the semester ended. In any case, it's too late. I am powerless to change their grades because those are the grades they earned. Again I wonder what kind of academic natural and logical consequences they experienced as second and third graders and through high school and college. They never learned the natural order of things. It may not be too early to ever start teaching children the academic facts of life, but I have seen many instances where it is certainly too late.*

A Word of Caution

Parents must exercise caution when allowing children to experience consequences in dangerous situations, as illustrated by the example of our daughter running across the street. When forgetting lunch, a child goes hungry but is not likely to starve to death. The child does remember to bring lunch the next day. Children should not, however, experience the consequences of an act that is obviously dangerous, the proverbial playing with fire, for example, or even crossing the street unattended. A toddler who touches the stove will learn from serious burns, but that of course is not what we are advocating. A demonstration from the warmth of the toaster may serve the purpose. Natural consequences must be used with discretion.

Very young children do not always understand that their actions affect the family, but they will learn in time. When our car stereo died, Bruce took our new van back to the dealer. The service attendant brought out the extracted stereo to demonstrate how spare change inserted into the tape deck had shorted out the unit. Our twins had turned the stereo into a $400 piggy bank. What one doesn't think of, the other one does. At least the stereo unit died a quick death. The van had two stereos—the one in the back had strawberry cookies fed to it. They realized the result next time they asked for their favorite tape to be played in the car.

At times, it may not be possible to teach children the natural consequences of their behavior, because of the risk or an unwillingness on the part of the child. With a little creativity, parents can devise a consequence logically related to misbehavior.

A mother in one of Kimberly's parenting classes had a five-year-old son who wanted to postpone his bath. His mother logically explained to her son that if he chose not to take a bath when the water was warm, he could choose to bathe later, even if the water was cold. He quickly decided that taking a bath in warm water was far better than in cold water, and his responsibility regarding bath time dramatically improved. After an appropriate age following potty training, children who choose to soil their pants should wash them out themselves. Teens who choose not to do family chores should not drive the family car until they pull their own weight around the house.

Implementing Order Through Consequences

As discussed previously, observing the rules of order is important to any organization. We strive for organization in the workplace and yet often leave order in the home to chance or convenience. It has been said that no success in life can compensate for failure in the home, yet how can the leader of a home hope to be successful in an unorganized one?

The pressures and time commitments of jobs and outside activities divert precious emotional resources from the most important organization—the family. We do what we can and then hope for the best, but the best never comes. When it doesn't, we become discouraged and angry toward our spouse and sometimes our children. Establishing order through natural and logical consequences to ensure the home's survival and success is in every family's best interest.

When implementing a program, it is often helpful to hold a family meeting to discuss the concepts of social order and respect for all. It may be a surprise to parents, but most children love the idea of increased choice and decision making within the family. It empowers! With older children, you can discuss the rise and fall of great civilizations that crumbled from within through disorganization and anarchy. For younger children, you can draw pictures of two houses—one that shows chaos, with family members yelling at each other; the other, orderly and happy. Then you can ask which home they would choose to live in.

Of course, children will choose the second. Explain that to achieve an orderly home, everyone needs to cooperate in changing the way things are done in the family. Within limits, decision-making responsibilities can be delegated to each family member concerned. When decisions affect the entire family, the group will collectively make a decision, with each family member allowed an equal voice. The idea is not to relinquish all power and decision making to the children—that would be permissive parenting. You are merely allowing them to participate in decision making for increased cooperation, responsibility, and self-esteem.

Basic Rules for Establishing Order

1. *Avoid performing any tasks your child can do for himself.* Often children become discouraged and refuse to accept responsibility because their high-functioning parents reject the child's efforts or redo the child's tasks to meet parental standards. High expectations are fine, but parents' perfectionist attitude can sometime be counterproductive. A family who was in therapy with Kimberly had a child that could never turn in an assignment without both parents redoing it to their satisfaction. Although the parents felt they were helping their son, it caused him to feel incapable and incompetent. He had quit trying—not

from laziness but from low self-esteem. He believed that his parents didn't trust him to do anything on his own.

As children take on new responsibilities, they may not initially perform to adult standards. At this stage, the effort is of most importance, not the end product. A child's self-image will not improve if parents do not believe the child will succeed. Parents must believe in their child and encourage every effort made, allowing the child to do the best he can. If your child has become accustomed to your doing things for him, he might resist change, demanding you continue to do things for him. Don't give in.

Kimberly relates:

Years ago I worked with a high-functioning couple whose child was born with several physical complica tions, requiring his parents to do things he could not do for himself. As he grew older, the parents continued to do these for him, even though the child had developed the physical ability to do them himself, such as cutting his own meat. By age 7, when he was referred to me by his pediatrician, he was emotionally only 4 or 5. After taking our parenting course, both parents refrained from doing things for their son. His emotional age increased dra matically as did his confidence. He proudly does whatev er he can for himself, with minimal help from his par ents. While maintaining an A average, this boy was recently voted fourth-grade class president by his peers.

Another family in therapy with Kimberly had parents who were looking for medical excuses for their child's tantrums. Instead of teaching their daughter to work through her negative emotion in a more positive way, they were searching for a diagnosis for a physical disease that would explain her tantrums and excuse them from responsibility. That seems incredible until we think of the rationale—it's a medical problem, not our problem.

2. *Refuse to allow the opinions of others to influence responsible parenting of your child.* Often we find that after parents change their parenting styles, they are bombarded with criticism from relatives, friends, neighbors, and sometimes even teachers. Grandparents feel defensive, believing that they raised you, the parent, correctly and can't understand why you should need to raise your own children differently. Others often expect the parents to help the child who can't, or *won't*, do for himself. They may hold parents accountable for everything the child does. Intimidated parents can take courage from realizing that children are independent beings who must learn to decide how they will behave and accept the consequences for their own behavior.

> Kimberly relates:
>
> *Johnny's third-grade teacher called his mother, my client, stating that he wasn't completing his homework and asking the mother what she was going to do about it. Mrs. Jones reacted by expressing embarrassment and anger with her son—concerned about what the teacher thought of her and her parenting of Johnny. Mrs. Jones stood over Johnny and forced him to do his homework only to learn that he was purposely discarding his home work papers on the way to school, an act of rebellion. After completing our class, in which she learned about natural and logical consequences, Mrs. Jones met with Johnny's teacher to discuss Johnny's responsibility for his own school behavior. The teacher began to understand that creating a battleground at home only increases a problem. The teacher and the mother together planned a discussion with Johnny to explain the consequences for his choices. During the ensuing weeks, Johnny chose to miss recess to complete his unfinished homework from the night before. At home, Johnny chose not to play with friends or participate in extracurricular activities until*

> *his school responsibilities were completed. Johnny soon became more responsible at school when others became less responsible for him.*

3. *Recognize who owns a problem.* As discussed in Johnny's case, many parents continue to assume ownership of problems that are actually their children's. Even when others try to make parents responsible for their children's problems, parents can extricate themselves by defining the problem, recognizing the owner, and then acting accordingly.

4. *Allow time for training.* Timing is everything when it comes to parenting children. The peak of a heated power struggle is not the time to discuss consequences and increased order in the home. A relaxed atmosphere, free from stress and time constraints, provides the ideal setting for encouraging and implementing order. We attempted to teach our son to tie his shoes one morning before school because we felt it was time for him to learn. The bus was coming and we were rushed. He felt pressured and we were more critical in our harried state when we needed to be encouraging. We had basically set ourselves up for failure, eventually giving up and tying his shoes for him. He became discouraged, and it was several weeks before he was willing to cooperate and try again.

    We have learned to plan ahead for experiences that are guaranteed to give our children success. We often need to modify our standards to make success even feasible. The clothes don't need to match perfectly if the child has made a sincere effort to dress himself. We take the time to train our children in household tasks to give them confidence to initiate the task on their own. Although a child can learn from the natural consequences of a mistake, it is equally important to plan adequate time for successes, which ensure self-confidence.

5. *Never pity your child.* In our failure, due to time constraints, to teach our son to tie his shoes, he ended up feeling pitied when we tied his shoes for him. Timing was everything in this instance because he was capable and would have succeeded had we allowed the time necessary for him to complete the task. Pity tells the child that he is somehow defective in handling problems. By overprotecting a child, an insecure parent gains a sense of strength and control by making the situation turn out right, but does so at the child's expense. Pity is not to be confused with empathy—sincere understanding of another's situation. Empathy promotes strength, whereas pity encourages weakness. When attempting to implement the appropriate consequence, many parents suddenly feel sorry for their child and then lessen the consequence or fail to follow through at all. This can cause the child to feel discouraged and fosters the very irresponsibility the consequence was intended to cure. Through the guilt reaction of their parents, children can also learn manipulation. Limits must be respected to create safe and appropriate boundaries for children.

6. *Ask—don't demand.* Demanding a child to perform a certain task decreases the child's desire and cooperation. On the other hand, a parent requesting a child's help in solving a problem appeals to children. It is a boost to a child's confidence to feel that a parent needs help to accomplish a task. A simple "I feel, I want" statement can enlist a child's cooperation—"I'm having a difficult time with this project, Ryan, and I really could use your help." If the parent-child relationship and respect have been established, the child will be anxious to help. If the child refuses, one of two things is occurring. As discussed in the chapter "Why Children Misbehave," if the parent feels hurt as a result of a refusal, the child is responding in revenge. The child is attempting to hurt the parent in retaliation for her hurt and rejection. Therefore it is best to accept the child's refusal of help and continue to work toward building the relationship. When

the relationship improves and the child chooses to help, appreciation should be expressed: "That helped me a lot, and it made my job easier."

Another reason for children's refusal to help is the result of permissive parenting. The child believes at the time that she is somehow better than the parent and deserves to be served. This selfishness in overpampered children can be handled by imposing a logical societal consequence to their behavior—stop serving them. When our children have chosen not to help us, we explain that although their *needs* will continue to be met, their *wants* won't be met until we feel better about the relationship. All extras, including rides to extracurricular events, stop until the child has improved the relationship with us. Children need to learn that respect is a two-way street.

Note that different consequences may need to be implemented for different children. Although some consequences are universally unpleasant—extra work, for example—others are not. One of our children absolutely hates to be sent to her room, while another loves the solitude—not much of a consequence for her. Sometimes our children resemble Brer Fox in the "Brer Rabbit" story—they plead, "Don't throw me in that briar patch," when in fact there is no place they would rather be sent. We have found in other instances that writing "I will not ..." fifty or one hundred times is effective with one child, but another child likes the challenge of seeing how fast he can do it. Even the consequence of cleaning additional rooms in the house is a much more pleasant task for our older daughter than spending time isolated from the family. Not that the rules are changed from child to child. The magnitude of the consequences should be the same, such as time taken to complete a task, but the actual consequence may need to be adapted from child to child. The adjustment can be dealt with effectively in weekly family meetings.

7. *Avoid power struggles by refusing to fight or give in.* As a parent, you provide choices and limits for your children. Therefore, you

must allow the child to decide how to respond to them. Be willing to accept the child's choice. There is no winning because there is no contest. The goal is to help children become responsible for their decisions; allowing them to experience the consequences for their choices is the first step.

Kimberly relates:

After teaching the concept of natural and logical consequences to a group of parents, several brought up examples of irresponsible behaviors of their children, which led to intense power struggles in the home. The goal of the group session was to help the others turn the power struggle into a choice for the child. One father was struggling with his son who had lost seven pairs of expensive prescription glasses. The group believed that letting the son pay for the glasses if he chooses to continue losing them would help him remember them. Two parents of a preschooler were even struggling in the session with each other about what to do with their child, who would not cooperate by getting dressed in the morning. Their own jobs were being jeopardized because of tardiness. The group consensus was to set a timer, and when it rang, she would have chosen to wear pajamas to school that day or clothes. This was difficult for the parents to agree to do because they feared the judgment of teachers and other parents if their daughter chose to oversleep and have to wear pajamas to school. A simple call to the teacher ahead of time helped this couple follow through with their daughter's choice. When we checked on the progress of the behaviors several weeks later, the son had become more responsible for his glasses, and after wearing her pajamas to school for one day, the preschooler was ready extra early the next day and the days that followed as well.

Our sons love to go to the grocery store with Bruce. The boys know that their chores must be completed before and there is frantic finishing of jobs often moments before their father leaves. Even though they all enjoy the trip, they sometimes choose to go and sometimes not, according to their choice of completing their chores. We do not nag them nor do we give in, even if they ask to complete chores upon returning home. We follow through with the consequence of their decision kindly but firmly. This exercise has taught them to be more responsible in carrying out their chores.

Another example in our family deals with issues of personal organization, which we have attempted to teach our children through the years. The children are responsible for cleaning their rooms before play, remembering their school books and homework, bringing their laundry to the washing machine by Saturday, and keeping their shoes in their shoe racks. When our children have chosen not to do these things, they suffer the consequences of poor organization. When their work is not completed and friends ask them to play, they miss out. When they forget their books and homework, they suffer the natural and logical consequence at school and have fewer privileges at home. When the laundry has been done on Saturday and they forgot to bring theirs to the laundry room, they do their own.

The Sunday morning routine can be hectic, to say the least. One Sunday, one of our older children chose to take her time getting ready for church and waited until the last minute to handle several personal details, including putting on her shoes. She assumed that her shoes were in the right place despite her disorganization—we can build the shoe racks as parents but can't make children use them. The five-minute warning before departure was given—no movement. Then the "everyone in the car" was sounded. Panicked, this child could not find one of her church shoes. She fretted, "I can't wear tennis shoes; what will the others think?" Our rule is you wear what you can put on when everyone walks out the door. That child wore her sneakers to church and the embarrassment encouraged shoe organization in the future. She cried and attempted to manipulate one of us to stay home until she found her shoe. We both declined because we felt it unfair for either parent to miss church.

The embarrassment was what this child needed to increase her responsibility. If we had been concerned more about our image as parents than about her character, this child would have been robbed of an important lesson. If we helped this child search for the shoe, we would have encouraged disorganization and laziness.

8. *Talk less when enforcing consequences and act more.* In the above example, it was important not to shame our child for her decision not to organize her shoes. It is tempting as parents to use the I-told-you-so attitude when children make mistakes by disregarding repeated warnings, but this breeds rebellion and hurts the parent-child relationship. Children learn best from the experience when we act, not react, to their irresponsibility. During a discussion with our daughter, she asked us why we were treating her like a terrible person. In an attempt to correct her, we had broken a rule by criticizing, which did not give her confidence that she could make right choices the next time. When implementing consequences, keep talk to a minimum as you follow through with action.

Bruce relates:

When I was varsity scout coach, my job was scout master to older boys, aged 14 to 17, who aspired to attain Eagle rank. I think a difficult temptation that parents should resist is pushing so hard in such a worthy cause that the Eagle rank ends up being "the toughest award my parents ever earned." I became an Eagle Scout at 14, thanks to supportive parents and advisers. The last four boys I worked with to attain their Eagle ranks were all 17. According to an experienced scoutmaster I know, it is easier to help the boys advance when they are young, before the scents of two "fumes" become important to them: perfume and gasoline fumes. Regarding the latter, I noticed that some parents in our troop began a simple policy: No Eagle rank, no driver's license. I was amazed at how effective this policy was. No power struggles, no lectures, no nagging. Eagle badge equals coveted plastic. It becomes even more effective when all the parents of boys in the troop or team have the same policy. Over the strenuous objections of our own sons, we have the same policy in our house. Although the oldest is only 12, he knows that in our family, only a boy responsible enough to earn his Eagle Scout rank is responsible enough to drive the family car.

9. *Let all the children share responsibility.* When family rules are violated in a group of siblings or one of children and friends, allow them all to experience the consequence equally. Faultfinding only increases rivalry among children and makes the parent the referee. Do not listen to tattling and let them decide how to handle the problem. In other words, do not get into the conflict. If you don't step in, but rather allow the children to keep the problem as their own, you will be surprised at how well the children will work it out in the future.

At one time, we had a problem with snack wrappers being left around the family room. We aired our frustration at a family meeting and decided that if the mess continued, there would be no snacks until increased responsibility for trash was exhibited. It was amazing how clean the family room became. Because we attempted to follow through every time, our children cooperatively made sure not to leave a mess and reminded siblings who forgot.

Another example surfaced when the table was a mess from snacks, Play Doh, and other children's activities. Around dinner hour, the children began to get hungry and asked about dinner.

Kimberly explained that she couldn't serve dinner on a messy table. Inspired by hunger, our daughter who sets the table told her brother who wipes it that he needed to wipe it first. Our 7-year-old table wiper, who was also hungry, asked our 4-year-old to clean up his Play Doh mess. Everything worked out fine. If they had chosen not to cooperate, a five-minute warning would have been given, and those who had completed their chores would have been allowed to eat.

Three Steps in Applying Consequences

1. *Propose the consequence in a choice form.* Alternative consequences/choices are proposed by the parent when the parent has a problem or when very young children in the family are treated unfairly. The family can discuss these consequence options collectively during family meetings. After the child's choice is made, the family accepts the child's decision. The parent's calm and matter-of-fact tone of voice when implementing the consequence is very important. An "I" statement at the onset of a discussion can let the child know what you are feeling and why a choice needs to be made.

2. *Assure the child that he or she can make a different choice later.* Children should not be punished and treated like "bad" children for making "bad" choices. They need to feel that they can choose differently and then have different, more positive results in the future.

3. *Increase the consequence if the choice is not acted upon.* If behavior violating another's rights continues, for example, yelling at siblings, the amount of time in time-out is increased before they may return to the family. Without an increase in time, the revolving-door effect occurs. Obviously parental "I" statements and the first time-out wasn't enough to discourage the behavior, so an increase of consequence or time-passing

needs to occur. The three-strikes-and-you're-out law (a third conviction of a violent crime mandates a life sentence) becoming popular in state legislatures is a result of criminals not learning a lesson by a short jail term on a first offense or a longer term on a second offense.

In disruptive talking, if the behavior continues even after they have chosen to return, the time needs to increase before they may again return. With disruptive behavior that violates parental rights, we often allow the child to decide when to return the first time, and we, as the parents, decide when to allow him to return the second time. If the child chooses to return and again disrupts our conversation, he knows that after making the choice to return and behaving badly again, the child temporarily loses the freedom of choice, and we choose when the child returns. As parents, we increase the time for a child to return until we at least finish our conversation, which motivates our children to choose more wisely when they have the opportunity again. This successfully encourages more responsible behavior.

As children learn to accept more responsibility for themselves and their behavior, they begin to enjoy their newly found independence. They gain confidence and a greater sense of identity and worth. Occasional periods of discouragement can be countered with encouragement and reminders of past efforts and tasks completed.

Rules to Remember

1. When you are not sure what you should do in any given situation, do nothing! Wait a few moments until you are certain of your course of action.

2. When implementing consequences, *act* rather than lecture. One consequence correctly implemented is worth a thousand lectures.

3. Learn to mind your *own* business—not your child's.

4. Treat your children with the dignity and respect you expect from them. Ask yourself, "How would I treat a close friend?" Make sure you then treat your child *at least* as well.

5. Be consistent. If the odds of getting away with misbehavior are better than hitting the lottery, it is no wonder children continue to misbehave. People continue buying lottery tickets.

6. Be firm but kind. Your tone of voice can turn a logical consequence into a punishment. Children often return your anger with theirs.

Nine

Consequences for Specific Challenges

As surely as the sun rises, you will face discipline challenges with your children. Dealing with small, daily problems when children are young will help prevent serious difficulties in children's teen years. In children, tantrums occur, which need to be dealt with. In adults, tantrums result from emotions not dealt with appropriately and from habits formed during childhood years. In Kimberly's therapy office, grown adults have thrown all-out, full-blown temper tantrums, the same as a 4-year-old in the supermarket. Tantrum-throwing adults are children who grew up with parents who did not administer natural and logical consequences.

As you have learned from previous chapters, natural and logical consequences encourage responsible behavior, whereas punishments that shame children lead to rebellion and contempt. According to the *New York Times*, teens today want parents to "explain the rules more and worry less." Natural and logical consequences accomplish just that, benefiting both parent and child.

Three Basic Rules

Parents must adhere to the following basic rules to apply natural and logical consequences successfully.

1. *Play It Straight.* There is no place for trickery or manipulation in natural and logical consequences. Hidden motives, such as control disguised as consequences, will backfire. The result can be the rebellion that consequences are meant to avoid. The ideas in this book should be discussed with your children. The honest intentions for better relationships and a happier family life should be explained.

2. *Avoid Power Struggles.* To implement natural and logical consequences effectively, you must learn to control your temper to set an example for your children. Any form of violence, inappropriate anger, punishment, and power struggle will poison your family's relationships.

3. *Stick With It.* These methods have worked for thousands of families. But usually success comes by tackling and overcoming one behavior at a time. Even when a problem is solved, relapses occur. Children will test the limits that have been established with consequences. This is termed the second offensive. Use the same procedure that worked the first time to handle a recurring problem, until the child learns that he will never hit the lottery by getting away with poor behavior.

Specific Challenge #1: The Morning Routine

In many families, getting all the kids up and ready for school can be a daily struggle. It can strain relationships and create resentment in parents who are doing too much for their children. Children will get up on time if they alone take ownership of the problem and face the consequences of being late. Nagging, coaxing, and goading only help reinforce the irresponsible behavior.

What to do:

1. Children over 5 years can be taught to use a simple alarm clock. Parents should take the child to the store to pick out a suitable model for the child to operate and then teach the child how to

set and use the clock. The child operates it, not the parents. If an alarm clock is not appropriate or practical, then one wake-up call from parents will substitute for the alarm.

2.   Teach children a system for preparing the next day's school clothes the night before. For very young children, pick out a couple of outfits and then let the child choose the next day's outfit.

3.   Teach children to attend to their own hygiene, such as hair care.

4.   Discuss the time breakfast will be available and when it will no longer be served. If a child misses breakfast, he or she will not starve, but will be there earlier the next day.

5.   Discuss the best time to wake up in the morning based on the time needed to dress, attend to hygiene, eat breakfast, and get to school on time. Have the child set the alarm for the time determined.

6.   From this point on, say nothing more about getting up and allow the child to experience the natural and logical consequences of oversleeping.

Example One: The Jones Family

After years of undergoing uncooperative mornings, Mrs. Jones taught her children to set alarm clocks, and together they established appropriate time frames for completion of all morning tasks. Her children's favorite part of the morning was breakfast, so breakfast time was set for 8:00. Her children could eat breakfast when they finished all their morning tasks. If they were not ready by 8:00, the children chose not to eat breakfast that morning, but could try again the next morning. Things ran smoothly the first week the Joneses tried this. During the following week, one child missed breakfast. Hunger helped him get back on his responsible routine the next day. Previous to implementing natural and logical consequences, Mrs. Jones would bring lunches to school when her children forgot them. She found that she was making constant trips to school to take lunches and other forgotten items. She now found that going hungry at lunchtime helped her children remember to take their lunches. With less time devoted to chasing after the children and correcting their irresponsible behavior, she now found time to do things she always wanted to do, such as continuing her schooling and enjoying her hobbies. Her children became more responsible in the process.

Example Two: The Thompson Family
When beginning his new plan to promote morning responsibilities, Mr. Thompson called his children's teachers to let them know that his children were now responsible for their mornings. When his children chose to be late to school, they chose to suffer school consequences. They did occasionally miss recess and lose other school privileges when they were late to school, which prompted more responsible behavior.

Our own children ride the bus to school. If it were not necessary to cross a freeway overpass, we would allow them to walk to school if they chose to miss the bus. Because walking is not a safe possibility, we have established a Mom & Dad taxi fee that must be paid if they miss the bus and we have to drive them to school. This fee, two dollars, is based upon our time expended and the gas used to drive them in our car since the car would not normally be driven for this purpose. Each child has paid the fee at least once and usually chooses to make the bus from then on. This same consequence also holds true for missing buses in the afternoon coming home from school.

The only time we allow our children to miss school is when they are sick. A few years ago, our son was slow to get ready, missed the bus, and then claimed he was not feeling well. Knowing that he was seeking extra attention, we explained that if he was sick, he would need to rest in bed until the next morning. After an hour in bed with no special attention, our son decided to return to school. The consequence of earning taxi money later that day and making up missed work during recess discouraged this behavior in the future.

When the parent assumes any responsibility for a child's morning routine, the child has no need to assume responsibility. The child will expect parents to continue the job of getting them ready for school. With well-positioned consequences in place, children will soon become tired of missed recesses, taxi fares, detentions, and staying home sick.

Specific Challenge #2: School Difficulties

Often parents become concerned about their children's school performance. This concern, an area over which the child feels should be his alone, can create a power struggle to the degree that we have actually seen children with genius intellect perform poorly on purpose. Lectures, comparisons to other children, and reiteration of past mistakes only accelerate the power struggle and strain relationships.

What to do:
1. If applicable, teach by example. It is the best way to inspire education and the freedom it provides. Take courses yourself through university extension programs or at the local community college. Do your homework in plain sight and discuss your courses.
2. At the table, discuss interesting, thoughtful subjects. Have a different topic for each meal. Search newspapers and magazines for discussion topics. Encourage your children to talk by listening to them.
3. Have magazines, encyclopedias, and reference material readily available to your children.
4. Never do a child's schoolwork for him. This has the opposite effect—children stop believing in themselves when you do. If a child requests help, assist him only in the challenge he absolutely cannot meet. If the child needs help to spell a word, direct her to a dictionary.
5. Do not reward a child for schoolwork completed or punish for uncompleted assignments. It is the child's business. He will learn that he can participate in his activities after he accomplishes home and school tasks. Show interest in the child's schoolwork and ask questions about it.
6. Become involved in your child's education. Join the PTA or vol-

unteer in the classroom. There are many ways of showing your interest and encouraging your child as well.

Kimberly relates:
James began doing poorly at school for the first time and seemed to have lost interest in his own education. His mother was an editor for a major magazine. When I questioned her, I learned that since the child's kindergarten year, she had redone her son's reports when he had finished them, believing she could do a better job. Her bright child's lack of interest in school stemmed from a lack of belief in himself—a direct result of improper parental involvement.

Consequences for Younger Children.
Study habits should be taught at a young age. Because school is a child's business, you assume your children will do their best at their job of school, just as you will do your best job as an adult. As a parent, you have certain responsibilities, too. If you did not perform to the best of your abilities, there would be a consequence for you. A working parent would be paid less or fired if he did not perform to the best of his abilities, and a parent who did not care for her children adequately might be considered neglectful by the authorities and could lose the children.

As parents, we can teach young children the importance of their twelve years of schooling by making time for study in the home. Our children should accomplish the things they need to do *before* doing the things they want to do. Homework and chores must be completed before extracurricular activities and fun. We assume they are doing their best, studying for their tests and completing their work appropriately, until we hear that they are not. Recently one of our children's teachers informed us that our child was choosing not to bring books home to study for tests, and the test grades reflected this lack of study. Because school is our children's responsibility and they are required to do their best, this child needed to cut back on TV viewing and on playtime with friends until the books were brought home and study increased. With this needed study, test scores naturally improved.

When our children come home with a 100 percent test or an A on a report, we reflect *their* excitement about *their* grades back to them. This encourages our children's natural desire to improve. The grades are theirs, not ours, we emphasize, and doing their best provides increased freedom, opportunities, and privileges for them while at home now and later in life. The patterns and good habits established while children are young will continue throughout their entire education, as will the bad habits without early intervention.

Consequences for Older Children.
Naturally, how you structure consequences for older children differs from methods for younger children, as with any behavior or parenting issue. The following examples demonstrate how to deal with older children and consequences.

Kimberly relates:
Although capable of much higher grades, a 15-year-old daughter who refused to study was getting F's in most of her classes. She was locked in a power struggle with her parents, and she knew grades were a way of lashing out at them. Because her parents had disapproved of her boyfriend and had restricted her from seeing him, the daughter had retaliated by letting her grades drop. Her parents questioned her repeatedly about her grades, forced her to study, and threatened at length. Although her parents forced her to do her homework, she chose not to turn it in. Her grades did not improve, and the parents were referred to me for the daughter's counseling.

When I initially met with the daughter and her parents, the power struggle over grades and boyfriend was evident. While I met with the teenager over the course of a few months, I made attendance at my parent education course mandatory for her parents. The daughter and I discussed probable outcomes of the choices she was making at school and the direction she was taking for the future, while her parents learned how to disengage from power struggles and help their daughter to become more responsible in her own life. After taking the nine-week course, the parents had a family meeting with all their adolescent children to discuss setting up a system for order in the home. School was their business. Homework completion would be their problem, and they were expected to do their best. Participating in extracurricular activities while failing at school would obviously detract from needed study time.

In establishing order, the family adopted the philosophy that we can't do the things we want to do until we accomplish the things we need to, or are required to do, in our jobs as parents and children. The parents also used "I" statements in this meeting to express their feelings of resentment if any of their children continued to fail in school after age 18 while still living at home. The father stated that he would resent providing financially for a child who chose to fail at his or her job while he, the father, was expected to succeed at his job and continue to provide support. A family law was established that any child over the age of 16 who chose not to do his best in school would then choose to provide financially for himself by getting a job to pay a percentage of rent and to provide for food and clothing.

All family members participated in the meeting. They voiced their concerns and eventually came to a consensus on fairness. It has been three months since this teen's parents took the parenting course. Her grades and attitude have improved dramatically. Loser friends are being replaced with motivated and more responsible ones. She is now talking about where to go to college and what to study there.

To summarize, one of the most serious mistakes parents can make is to become overinvolved in their children's education when they are doing their best. Nagging and coercing decrease motivation. Overdoing for children creates insecurity and laziness. Parents should begin when children are young to motivate them indirectly by creating an intellectual atmosphere and establishing a time to study before extracurricular activities are pursued. If you value and participate in educational pursuits, your children most likely will as well. School should be the child's business and it will be if you allow it and require it.

Specific Challenge #3: Household Chores

To establish true order in a home, all members must participate in both the work and the fun. Raising responsible children requires parents to give their children chores to learn responsibility. When establishing chores at age 4 or 5 for our younger children, we often tell the story of the Little Red Hen. They can relate to the frustration of the hen when her friends are not willing to help make the bread and yet expect to eat it anyway.

After the story is related, usually at the family meeting, all chores that need to be done are listed, and family members choose the chores they prefer doing. Usually everyone gets their first or second choices. When the least favorite chores are left, we rotate them on a monthly basis so that everybody shares the burden. A time is established (sometimes for each child individually, depending on school schedules) for all chores to be accomplished. Before dinner is a good time, since we can't eat the food until it is provided for. Television, computer fun, and play definitely do not occur until chores and homework are completed.

Often unpleasant chores such as cleaning bathrooms and taking out garbage present a problem for some families. Sadly, autocratic parents devalue their children and give them unpleasant tasks that the parents themselves choose not to perform. This assignment shows children that they have a lowered family status. Rebellion in some form usually follows. When children are allowed to participate in chore allocation and rotation, cooperation follows.

The following example from Kimberly's practice probably best illustrates how to solve the problem of getting every family member to pitch in with household chores.

Kimberly relates:

Recently a single mother came to my office with her two uncooperative 6- and 9-year-old daughters. She stated that she felt overwhelmed, working all day and coming home to more work and ultimate exhaustion. Both daughters to this point had chosen to be uncooperative, and any effort to force them to help ended in major power struggles. While meeting with all three, I first related the story of Little Red Hen and asked why this story was similar to their home. The youngest, grinning, answered, "Mommy does all the work." I asked the mother how she felt about that, while coaching her to use the "I" statement format. She stated that she feels overwhelmed by the workload and hurt and resentful that she doesn't have any help from her daughters. She even stated that she had reached the point where she did not like spending time with them and did not feel like doing special things for them.

The girls were shocked to hear these feelings from their mother. Typically, they had ignored her yelling and spanking at chore time and were now surprised to learn of her feelings. A renewed respect for mother was established, and the daughters apologized for their lack of cooperation. We began with a mini-family meeting, brainstorming about all the jobs there were to do around the house. This family unit had six general home jobs and six dinnertime jobs.

General Jobs:
1. *Sorting and washing clothes*
2. *Folding clothes*
3. *Vacuuming and dusting common areas*
4. *Cleaning bathroom*
5. *Removing trash*
6. *Cleaning animal cage*

Dinnertime Jobs:
1. *Setting the table*
2. *Clearing and washing the table*
3. *Sweeping floor*
4. *Washing dishes*
5. *Rinsing dishes*
6. *Putting away dishes*

Once all jobs were listed, everyone felt it was fair to choose four jobs each (two general chores and two dinnertime chores). As I named each job, the three were to choose that job or another. Each got their first and second choice of the general chores. The younger (formerly, the least coopera-tive daughter) thought of another job she wanted to add, making her total three for that category. This is not that amazing when children are part of the decision-making process. Cooperation above and beyond the call of duty typi-cally results.

When choosing the kitchen chores, both girls wanted the same job, so a tie-breaking method had to be selected. Although it took five minutes to agree, consensus was finally reached by picking a number between one and ten. Since they had all decided on the method of tie breaking, there were no sad faces when the winner was named. Everyone decided that these chores would be rotated every two weeks so that they all would have the chance to do their favorite chore and a fair turn at their least favorite.

The older child brought up the issue of allowance and felt she should be paid for her work at home. I asked her what she felt would be fair and an amount was discussed. The amount negotiated was not for cleaning her room or doing her homework—those things are her responsibility solely. The money allowance would be her share from the family chores she helped perform. From her allowance, she would pay for things she wanted. If she requested something extra at the market, her mother would ask her if she had brought her money with her. If she forgot her money or had none, she would suffer the consequences of not being able to buy what she wanted, like anyone else.

Extra money for expensive purchases would need to be contracted for and earned by accomplishing extra jobs. No one would be eligible to do extra contracted jobs until her regular assigned jobs were completed. The mother left my office with the task of making a list of additional jobs with a monetary value attached to each one. The girls were encouraged to assist. For example:

Cleaning oven—$1.00

Washing windows—$.25 each

Pulling weeds in back yard—$2.00

Mopping floors—$1.50

Washing walls—$2.00

This family was well on its way to establishing order in household chores with logical and natural consequences.

The obvious consequence for children who do not complete their jobs is to forfeit doing what they want until they finish their assigned jobs. Nagging and threats are eliminated when children see that they can't play or watch television until their designated work, established at a family meeting, is completed.

Two systems have proven effective when dealing with chores and allowance. The first system, for younger children, is based on the child's ability to responsibly remember his or her tasks and to accomplish them without nagging or coercion. Allowances for family chores completed are paid once a week. The children are paid per day for jobs accomplished. On any day that reminders are given, children are not paid for that day. An employer might give a written warning for such behavior in a work setting and after too many warnings terminate the employee. Although they must accomplish their jobs each day before they do what they *want* to do, they are paid only when they remember to do them on their own and do them well. Each day is worth a percentage of the total allowance given each week, with money deducted accordingly. At a family meeting, we offer to make a job list for their bedroom doors to help them remember their responsibilities. For our youngest children yet unable to read, we create job charts with pictures, such as a cat for feeding the cat.

Even though our children know they are not to play or do other things they want to do until their chores are completed, they sometimes forget. When they watch television before work is done, they automatically do not watch television the next day. This logical consequence reminds them to do what they are supposed to do before doing what they want to do. If they forget again within the same week, then it becomes two days without television or without playing with friends.

Different criteria for completing each job are established and a parent typically does the job initially with the child. Any questions about the job and its completion are to be asked at that time. From then on, if a family member chooses to do a job sloppily, requiring a parent to point out a negligent error, that family member must do an extra job because of the extra parent effort expended. On the other hand, we give a bonus at the end of a great week when no reminders are given and jobs are done thoroughly.

The second system, for older children, relies on the fact that most older children can remember their chosen chores and know how they are to be done. When they choose not to do the chore in the allotted time frame, it still has to be done to keep order in the home. The child who did not accomplish his chore must pay an agreed-upon amount to a parent or another family member to do it. Jobs are up for grabs to anyone after the time set passes. Dinner cannot be cooked in a dirty kitchen and the table cannot be set onto a dirty table. The child becomes more cooperative with his chores after paying family members overtime for the jobs he should be doing.

Children become more responsible, independent, and confident when tasks are shared at home. Children who do not share tasks become selfish, presumptuous, and unadaptable to a work environment later in life. Allowances help children to learn the value of money and how to handle it at an early age. Our children save 10 percent of their earnings in their bank accounts.

Specific Challenge #4: Bedtime

Most parents have difficulty getting their children to go to bed at night. Children may resist going to bed for various reasons. Some children feel that they are not tired at the parental designated hour or don't want to miss out on any fun. Some want more attention while others may seem fearful for one reason or another. If orchestrated ahead of time, bedtime can be fun and a special time for parent and child to look forward to, a time for bonding.

For Younger Children
Although no one can force a child to sleep, establishing a bedtime routine and forming the habit of staying in bed until falling asleep is crucial. The routine must be kept simple and regular. Specific bedtimes can be established at the weekly family meeting, discussed in the next chapter. When bedtimes are negotiated to fit an individual child's needs, children tend to cooperate more readily.

If your children typically bathe in the evening, bath time can be the first signal that the bedtime ritual has begun. Children who can read the hands on the clock can be alerted to bedtime by this method. Young children watching television can be signaled to prepare for bed by particular shows. Darkness is not a good signal because it changes with the seasons and daylight savings time, which confuses children.

A bedtime routine should include the following rituals.
1. Bath
2. Putting on pajamas
3. Teeth brushing
4. Story time
5. Prayers
6. Preparations for morning: laying out clothes
7. Sharing time with parent
8. Good-night hug and kiss

Make certain you end at the agreed-upon time or after the habitual ritual. Don't allow guilt from the day to cause you to stray from routine. Your children will learn to manipulate you, causing your resentment. End the routine with a hug and a kiss. If your child typically uses unwarranted night fears to detain you, your response is crucial. Give brief reassurance—"Good night. You'll be fine." These are usually attention-getting behaviors; even fears can be used to get attention, often subconsciously. If your child wakes in the night, the attention should be kept to a minimum. Otherwise the child may feel that the parent wouldn't be paying so much attention if there really wasn't something to fear. After waiting a minute or two, say *briefly* that it was a bad dream. After saying good night, leave the room. Any extra attention will encourage nightmares to continue.

Any routine devised needs to be consistent and special. The bedtime routine is the last thing your child experiences before he drifts off to sleep. His dreams, whether positive or negative, can be affected by the routine—make it organized and positive.

Natural and logical consequences for failing to follow the routine or refusing to go to bed thereafter can be implemented as follows. First, avoid power struggles. Explain to the child that if she chooses to not go to bed, she will miss part of the routine the next night. Another option could be going to bed earlier the next night, depending on the time wasted tonight. A rule of thumb we use is fifteen minutes for every disturbance after bedtime.

For Older Children

Older children can establish appropriate bedtimes/curfews with parents during the family meeting. Parents can assume that after the appointed time, the children are to be home, preparing for bed. If curfews are not kept, the child chooses to stay home the following night. This grounding compounds as the child continues to disregard the set curfew. For example, the next time he misses curfew, he chooses to stay home for two nights, and so forth.

Often there are consequences at school when a child oversleeps, usually from inadequate sleep during the night. Poor grades, detention from recess help children to remember to be more responsible at bedtime and get to school on time. Somewhere between the ages of 8 and 10, bedtime routines become less important, and children need to be responsible for getting to bed on time.

If older children disrupt their parents at all after the appointed bedtime hour, then an FAB needs to be sent. "I feel irritated that you are watching a TV show in my room past your appointed bedtime because I need my space, too. I would like you to go to your own room." If the child remains, the consequence of an earlier bedtime the next night to make up for the parent's lost "space-time" should be discussed.

Specific Challenge #5: Disrespect for Parents

Sooner or later, children will try to exert their independence. If channeled correctly, this effort can help children become responsible adults. Unfortunately, sometimes independence translates into disrespect for parents. This can take many forms, but usually surfaces harmlessly as a flippant remark or, more seriously, shouting and yelling—an older child's version of a tantrum.

In this situation, as in other challenges, the democratic principles of family life and mutual respect should be applied. The parent cannot react too permissively by allowing the behavior to continue, but yet must make it clear without becoming abusive that such behavior is unacceptable. For younger children, a time-out might do, stating, "When you are ready to calm down, you may return to the family." A specific amount of time, say twenty minutes, also works well, but the consequence should be decided in advance in the set of family rules. If the child returns from time-out still storming, he has proven unable or unwilling to discipline himself, so the parents then decide when the child can return.

For older children who talk back, ask, "If you talked like that to one of your teachers at school or your principal, what would happen?" They acknowledge, if not begrudgingly, that they would be in big trouble. "If it is not acceptable at school, it is not acceptable at home." Children need to realize that respect for parental authority is just as important as respect for educational authority or the legal authority of a police officer or judge. Not that parents are cops, as discussed previously, but parents are charged by society in a legal and moral sense with the responsibility of raising children. With responsibility comes authority, which cannot be abused, but must be respected. Just because the authority figure happens to dwell in the same household doesn't mean there should be less respect.

With older children, the time-out concept can take different forms and still be effective, although actual separation from family or friends can work. With our teenage daughter, for example, restricting her time with friends at parties or other activities is the ultimate punishment. It's a social time-out. We use social time-out not as an arbitrary punishment but as a natural and logical consequence for not choosing to be respectful to parents. "If you can't control yourself enough to be nice to us, you can't have the opportunity to be nice to your friends. We deserve kind treatment as much as they do." We feel that family relationships should and do come first. Fighting among older siblings can be handled in much the same way: "If you can't be kind to your family members, you can't go off to have fun with your friends." Many times after children have quarreled with siblings, they ask to go over to a friend's house. It is extremely effective to deny the request with the consequence of social time-out.

Ten

The Overdiagnosed Attention Deficit Disorder

Attention Deficit Disorder, ADD (sometimes called ADHD, or Attention Deficit Hyperactivity Disorder), is without question one of the hottest, most controversial parenting topics of our day. We feel this issue is so timely that it deserves some special explanation and understanding as a chapter in this book. We believe that the secret to ADD is a lack of natural and logical consequences implemented by caregivers and a lack of impulse control exhibited by children.

We are not conspiracy theorists. We don't believe that all pediatricians, teachers, and administrators are all in on the ADD game, trying to fleece parents out of their money while ridding the world of undesirable children. For one, we don't know all the health and education professionals in the world; in addition, our experience, as well as yours, would indicate that the vast majority are caring, competent people. In our limited scope of experience, however, we are amazed and troubled by general trends emerging—trends that credible research has begun to validate: The ADD diagnosis just doesn't hold up in too many cases; therefore, the ADD picture just doesn't add up.

"The Biological Devil Made Me Do It"

ADD is one of the fastest-growing diagnostic categories in the medical community for children and surprisingly adults as well. Prescriptions for Ritalin, the drug of choice for this so-called disorder, have risen more than 300 percent in just four years, according to a *Time* magazine cover story article. "A lot of people are jumping on the bandwagon," complains psychologist Mark Stein, director of a special ADD clinic at the University of Chicago. "Parents are putting pressure on health professionals to make the diagnosis." But it's not just parents that are pressuring. Many schools and educators have jumped on the ADD bandwagon as well. With class sizes increasing and many parents passing the discipline of their children to schools, teachers and administrators are confronted with indulged, disruptive children. All too often teachers are making the diagnosis themselves, encouraging parents to put their children on medication. Sometimes parents are all too glad to comply, hearing justification, from a professional, no less, for imposing outside intervention with their problem child.

In Kimberly's practice and in our school and community in general, we are amazed at how quickly educators pressure parents if their child fits any part of a ten-symptom model devised for diagnosing ADD and ADHD. "It says here 'Likes to play with older children'— there you have it—must be ADD." We have heard similar words first-hand from teachers. Parents then feel obligated to seek the school-recommended medication from their doctor, fearing less than fair treatment of their child by the school if they do not comply—"The teacher said so, so we had better do it." We've heard these words, too, from parents. There have been teachers that even go so far as to pressure students by asking if they have seen a physician yet and, if not, asking the parents when they will schedule an appointment. Have parents lost their sense of healthy suspicion? By what reason do gym teachers have the ability and training to diagnose a mental health condition? If parents are not asking themselves this question, they should ask it at the highest levels of academic administration in their child's school and in the district. Six of ten parents in the United States believe it's not permissible for a teacher to spank a child. Why would those same parents let a teacher "strongly suggest" that a child be put on Ritalin, which probably has much more far-reaching consequences? We hope to soon see a backlash against trigger-happy educators, which will bring some well-needed balance to the issue.

We asked a school principal how many students at the school were on Ritalin. The principal responded that about 25 percent were. Since the rate of what scientists call "true" ADD is about 2 percent, we wondered aloud if something in the community's water system is causing the difference. We suspect that the difference is instead overwhelmed parents and overworked teachers, both of whom are genuinely concerned, but have simply not wanted to take effective discipline to a higher level of priority in their lives or profession.

The allure of ADD for all concerned is that it is "a label of forgiveness," says Robert Reid, an assistant professor in the department of special education at the University of Nebraska. "The kid's problems are not his parents' fault, not the teacher's fault, not the kid's fault. It's better to say this kid has ADHD than to say this kid drives everybody up the wall." For adults, the diagnosis may provide an excuse for personal or professional failures, observes Richard Bromfield, a psychologist at Harvard Medical School. "Some people like to say, 'The biological devil made me do it.'"

This excuse theory of ADD holds true for another biological devil frequently used as an excuse for teens today: hormones. Teens and many parents use this excuse to avoid responsibility for actions less than appropriate or responsible. We recall attending a middle school orientation with our daughter a few years ago where the school counselor was discussing the issue of hormones and behavioral changes in teenagers. The counselor began excusing poor school performance, disrespect to parents, and other inappropriate behaviors as a normal teenage stage to be expected. Our daughter, to her credit at the time, turned to us in disgust, questioning what kind of children the counselor must be seeing. We left almost immediately.

However, since this behavior was subconsciously excused for all teens in attendance, we began to see these behaviors surface in her within days after the orientation. We were shocked! She cited further excuses—in addition to the counselor's remarks, her textbooks and class notes from her health teacher—all in the name of hormones. Enough was enough. At our family's next meeting, these behaviors were identified and categorized. Specific consequences were planned if the behaviors surfaced in anyone in our home.

Attention Deficit or Effort Deficit?

In Kimberly's therapy work with children who have been wrongly labeled with ADD, she constantly hears the ADD excuse for normal day-to-day tasks. "I didn't do well on that test because I forgot to take my Ritalin that morning." When questioned whether the teen had studied for the test, "Well, not really" is the reply. It is a lack of effort and self-discipline, not a lack of attention, that explains the child's poor performance. Ritalin, Dexadril, and other medications cannot conjure up test information in a child's head that wasn't there in the first place. These children are usually so bright and creative that they quickly figure out what is needed to get by, and they do nothing more than that. They assume they have learned the system and ways to beat it. However, they discover, sometimes too late, that beating the system with their lack of effort only beats themselves in the long run. Wrongly attributing lack of effort to ADD, by children, parents, or teachers, cheats kids of learning the social order of life and necessary work ethic for survival. Some parents may find the prospect of supporting their adult children financially appealing, but we do not. Unfortunately, here is a familiar refrain from some parents: "Well, you see, he's been diagnosed with ADD, so we've got him on Ritalin …. We're doing all we can…" It may be that they are doing all they know about. Trying a different parenting approach could probably make a difference.

Many children choose the subjects in which they will apply effort. Subjects that interest them get the requisite effort and those that don't get little or none. Teachers and parents complain of a child's inconsistency in school performance. And because this is one symptom for a diagnosis of ADD, parents are encouraged by many teachers to medicate their child to help him become a more consistent student—especially a child who tests well in national or intellectual testing. Rather than medicate a child for inconsistency, parents and educators need to teach children that we don't always get to do what we like to do in life. Sometimes there are duties in our adult jobs that we don't necessarily like but must do because they are part of the job. On a more basic level, there are unpleasant household jobs that no one likes to do, such as cleaning the toilets, but they must be done. Few people would think of putting their kids on Ritalin because they don't like to clean toilets, but the scholastic and academic equivalent is precisely what happens in an ADD my-kid-needs-more-consistency diagnosis.

We all complain that in many ways, school is not like the real world. But in other ways, school is very much like the real world. There are days you must do things that are no fun at all. This is something parents must teach and children must learn. Performing well in all subjects in school is a child's job as a student. We all have jobs to perform. As discussed in the chapter "Consequences That Create Responsibility," just as a parent or teen would be fired from a job for poor performance, so should a child be stripped of extracurricular activities (optional) by not performing consistently in his job, which is to be the best student he can be (required).

Privileges such as television, video games, and even bedtime routines can also depend on effort put into the child's main job—a student. Another natural consequence to poor school performance can be redoing any papers or homework in which the best effort was not applied. This consequence should encourage any child's best effort the first time to avoid expending more effort a second time. We say, "If you don't have time to do it right the first time, you have to make the time to do it over." Effort is important here—not the grade. Bright children can often get high grades without much study. But that does not qualify as best. Best is their best effort, and their teachers are usually well aware of when best effort is put forward and conversely, can inform parents when it is not. You as parents can also judge. Did you see the child studying for that high-graded test or working on the project? Though children can often get high grades with little or no effort in elementary school, these low effort habits hurt them later when grades really count and classes are much tougher.

Accountability

An easy accountability system is outlined below. Children who are not putting forth their best effort are required to bring this sheet to each of their teachers. The teacher must sign it, check whether all homework was turned in, and give a rating of 1 through 10 for the effort expended that particular week (10 being best effort). Pass/fail on effort might also be used.

Subject	Teacher's Signature	Homework	Effort Level
1.			
2.			
3.			

If the child does not have teachers complete the form for the week, privileges and opportunities are withheld until the next reporting period. This holds true even if the child claims it was completed, but the wind blew it away or the neighbor's dog ate it on the way home.

Often, brilliant but lazy children test extremely well on IQ tests or do well when no effort is required on coursework or quizzes. Teachers and parents can't understand why Junior performs below his ability level until they realize that Junior doesn't have to. He isn't fired from his job as student or neglected as a child because of his lack of effort and self-discipline. In fact, he continues to enjoy three wonderful meals a day, has a comfortable place to live, and wears all the name-brand clothing a kid could want—and a psychiatric diagnosis is his excuse. We think that the trouble with labeling kids with a psychiatric diagnosis is just that—they are labeled for life. We believe it—

they believe it, too, whether accurate or not. Children need to experience the consequences for their behaviors, good and bad, from a young age. If they don't, they get a false and distorted image of the world and will be at a loss to function in it appropriately as an adult. Interviews with prison inmates reveal that most criminals do not think their actions will land them in jail. They don't believe they will get caught, because they did not suffer appropriate consequences as children. Consistency and accountability for every choice make all the difference for a child in the effort-deficit mode.

Another example of lack of effort in the classroom is the child assigned to summer school for poor school performance during the regular school year. This is the way the public schools show children that if they choose not to do their best during the regular school year, they can spend their vacation time during the summer making up work. Even if schools don't assign your effort-deficit child to summer school, a parent can request a textbook from a class in which their child applied low effort. The child can then spend several hours each day during the summer repeating the class, thereby catching up in what they could have and should have learned during the normal school year. Making children accountable for low effort in school helps them put forth the necessary effort needed in their future.

Hyperactive Parenting

Too often it is the parent, not the child, whose hyperactivity spawns the ADD symptoms and diagnosis. We discussed overinvolved parenting briefly in the chapter "Birth Order and Behavior." Well-meaning parents take responsibility for everything their children do, perhaps believing that their child's performance reflects on their own competence as parents. Hyperactive parents are also created when their children receive the diagnosis of ADD, believing that their children are now incapable of managing their own lives. ADD also excuses their child from making any effort on his own because he can't with a disease that renders them helpless. These parents coax, nag, and coerce their children. This parental effort allows the child to expend less effort on her own behalf. When a hyperactive parent continually reminds a lazy child when his assignments are due, when to do them, and often how to do them, why should the child put forth any mental energy of his own to take responsibility? As discussed previously, when parents become less responsible for their children's school work, the children have to become more responsible themselves—that is, if the children want any activities except their job as a student.

Stimulation Deficit

"School is boring and unstimulating" is what Kimberly hears from very bright children and their parents referred to her practice for ADD reasons. Typically, these children are extremely bright, but need to be challenged. A classroom need not be overcrowded to cause difficulty in meeting the intellectual levels of all children enrolled. Boredom might be a reason for a gifted child's daydreaming or other bad habits, but such behaviors can stem from an initial lack of interest, which does not and cannot excuse negative behaviors. It's not fair to the teacher or to the other children. Stimulation-deficit children need to learn how to work with their teachers and parents to find intellectual activities when class work is completed instead of bothering other students or tuning out in the classroom. If stimulation in the classroom is a problem with your child, notify your child's teacher and discuss how best to meet your child's individual needs.

Self-Discipline Deficit

Psychologists Edward Hallowell and John Ratey in their best-selling book *Driven to Distraction* suggest that American life is ADD-ogenic: "American society tends to create ADD-like symptoms in us all. The fast pace. The sound bite. The quick cuts. The TV remote-control clicker. It is important to keep this in mind, or we may start thinking that everybody you know has ADD." True words indeed.

In our fast-paced society, we find many parents and children who crave instant gratification and are confused by needs and wants. Not that marketing and selling are the root of all evil, but a free-market economy with its enticing advertising drives many of us to seek everything we want, thinking we really need it. An age-old debate in schools of business is whether marketing creates demand or merely informs the consumer of what is available. Anyone who has ever watched Saturday morning cartoons with a child knows that advertising creates demand! Teaching ourselves and our children the difference between material needs and wants is crucial if we are to survive as a functional society and as families. In addition, distinguishing between activity needs versus wants is important. Learning to do what we *need* to do before doing what we *want* to do is as important for parents as for their children.

In Kimberly's southern California practice, she saw many adolescents who were in some form of depression because their family wasn't keeping up with the Joneses. This destructive pattern of self-indulgence diverts attention from important priorities like our marriages and our duty to discipline ourselves and our children. Children and now adults are frequently medicated unnecessarily when only a change of habits and structure is needed. In addition to negative stigma, many children with whom Kimberly has worked are drugged unnecessarily and don't like the thought of taking mind-altering drugs when they believe there should be other alternatives to their bad habits. The concepts of order and discipline taught in this book can help parents make the necessary changes.

Structure Deficit

Of the two parenting styles—permissive and autocratic—permissive parenting produces the majority of cases of ADD and ADHD. In permissive homes, little or no limits are set or reinforced. Bad habits and impulses flourish unchecked. Creativity and distractions abound with little or no structure, which ultimately leads to lack of control over most impulses. Many parents who have avoided the ADD label for their preschool children nonetheless tell us that their child's habits, which are creating a lack of order in their home, are merely a stage he is going through. When Kimberly explains that she counsels 35-year-olds who throw tantrums, parents often begin to look at their child's behavior in terms of lack of structure and discipline.

Take, for example, children who were not structured into a potty-training routine. They are often labeled with the psychiatric diagnosis of encopretic or enuretic, with a secondary diagnosis of ADD. When they enter therapy with depression from such impulse control difficulties, we end up going back to a lack of potty-training structure, which should have been in place from the age of 3. All that's required is age-appropriate structure often implemented through creative discipline techniques. Without such structure, children continue bad habits into later childhood and then find it difficult to stop after years of no impulse control. That is what leads to embarrassment and ultimately depression.

Kimberly relates:

Several years ago, a young girl was referred to me by her medical doctor for soiling herself at age 10 (after age 5, this type of soiling is known as encopretic behavior). She had been diagnosed with ADD and was taking Ritalin. Her mother had excused the soiling behavior, attributing it to the divorce from her husband that occurred when her daughter was 4 years old. Jennifer was never expected to use the toilet on her own, so she often soiled her underwear. Though she always carried spare underwear and a plastic bag for accidents at school, this posed a problem for her at age 10 because she now desired to spend the night with friends and she feared embarrassment.

Mother had excused Jennifer from potty training because of the daughter's divorce anxiety. Fearing further trauma to Jennifer, her mother imposed little structure or limits in other areas of Jennifer's life as well. Jennifer also bounced back and forth between both parents, who shared custody. Half the week was spent with one parent and half with the other. Consistency in parenting seemed almost impossible. Lack of structure caused Jennifer to be suppressed in many areas of her life, but she was seldom held responsible for many age-appropriate tasks. Because the lack of structure

had continued for so for many years, Jennifer actually
believed that she could not perform the tasks that most other
children could.

Many well-meaning but permissive parents explain that they would like to wait until their child wants to be trained. It is true that some children desire to establish their own independence by potty training themselves or at least initiating it. Sadly, there are just as many children who think that eliminating in training pants is much more convenient for them. Why ever be potty trained? After all, there is always a new supply of these free fresh wonders and mom or dad can clean up the mess. Much of the depression in children and adults Kimberly has treated over the years can be traced to bad habits due to the lack of structure and self-discipline in their lives—bad habits resulting too frequently from permissive parenting. The world has its share of permissive parents and distractible kids, but the rest of the world treats these behavior problems as behavior problems rather than diseases. France and England report one-tenth the U.S. rate of ADD.

We discussed in the Introduction the idea of the pendulum of parenting styles again swinging back to an autocratic model, as educators and parents are now calling for more discipline in the schools and in the home. The corporal punishment and autocratic styles of the early twentieth century may eliminate attention deficit behaviors, but may also stifle creativity and self-esteem as well. More schools would probably use corporal punishment if they could, and the topic is the issue of debate in many districts. Teachers feel overwhelmed with their increasingly impulsive student population and have few options to deal with this problem. Ritalin seems to be the answer—it controls without a paddle. It subdues impulsive students and their disruptive behaviors. It also removes the responsibility of behavior from the student, the parent, and the teacher, since the child's impulses vanish. When we visit our kids at school for lunch, the line at the nurse's office seems to be getting longer.

Most of the ADD children Kimberly has seen in therapy both in California and South Carolina don't want the ADD label. They and their parents are often opposed to taking a drug but feel pressured to do so. After implementing the structure that democratic discipline encourages, many children's ADD-like behaviors and habits disappear—not from the miracle of Ritalin. Far from it. It's the discipline of applying consistent, sensible parenting to which children respond. However, more than once, we know of a teacher or principal who has gone so far as calling a child's doctor to continue the medication. The educators fear that the symptoms will return.

Security Deficit

As mentioned in the chapter "Why Children Misbehave," divorce can elicit a wide range of behavioral symptoms in children. No wonder many of the children with ADD symptoms referred to Kimberly's practice come from divorced or divorcing families. The divorce transition for a child can cause much anxiety. A child in this situation should not be misdiagnosed with ADD or drugged unnecessarily. Children going though this experience should be taught coping skills, not escaping skills.

Child psychiatrist Larry Silver of Georgetown University Medical Center stated that the most common misdiagnosis of ADD he sees is anxiety. A child worried by a problem at home or some other matter can look hyperactive and distractible. Family sessions and brief individual psychotherapy often abate these hyperactive-like symptoms as quickly as they surface. As stated before, consistency in parenting to provide impulse control and a balanced healthy family life is the key.

The Real Cure

In Irvine, California, 45 children attend the Child Development Center, a kind of experiment in progress with ADD kids. Only 35 percent of the kids are on stimulant drugs, less than half the national rate for ADD children. Given their symptoms of impulsiveness and lack of control, these children are provided more structure and consistency than other schools. At the center, appropriate behaviors are encouraged by giving greater privileges to higher scorers on tests, as they demonstrate their increased responsibility. Children define their goals and take orderly steps to reach them.

The program works because it provides a balance of creativity and structure with consistency—things achieved in a functional/ democratic home. Drugs aren't needed as habits change and children learn to focus their energies appropriately. Unfortunately, most public schools are overcrowded and do not train their teachers in any type of behavior management, which results in hyperactivity in schools.

Many school districts are now spending tax dollars to train their teachers to spot cases of ADD more readily. This is a scary trend. Fed up with impulsive children and undisciplined parents, schools are fighting back with diagnosing children themselves and pressuring parents to ask their doctors to medicate. It's an attempt to maintain order in chaotic classrooms. Unethical and unnecessary in many cases, it nonetheless happens every day in this country.

ADD traits are not always disabling. Children raised in democratic homes in which children make decisions for themselves within the framework of order often exhibit traits that include risk-taking, creativity, and nonlinear thinking. They lack compulsivity and have a balance of structure.

Adults who were children raised without autocracy are often not satisfied with a single professional pursuit and are often characterized as Renaissance men, masters of many arts. History is replete with men like Benjamin Franklin and Thomas Jefferson—statesmen, scientists, philosophers, writers, connoisseurs. These men probably exhibited some of the restlessness of thought and action that gets slapped with the ADD label today.

ADD is not an epidemic. It is a warning. In time, ADD children grow up to excuse whatever goes wrong in their lives or their failures with "I was an ADD child." Permissive parents need to provide more structure for their children's creativity, and autocratic parents need to stop muzzling it. Both permissive and autocratic parents limit children's creativity and self-esteem. What is needed is less diagnosis and more parenting that engenders responsibility and self-respect in children. This will do more than any drug to cure the ADD disorder, especially since it is so often misdiagnosed. Far too often, attention deficit is nothing more than deficits in effort, stimulation, self-discipline, structure, or security, which can be cured with more attention to parenting, not a prescription for Ritalin.

Eleven

Holding Family Meetings

You ou know you have a lot of kids when you don't feel the 5.0 earthquake in California because there's a 6.0 going on in the house, or when you leave an extra big tip for the huge dinner mess and then quietly leave your table—at home! Unfortunately, the challenges and issues we face don't work themselves out as in a thirty-minute sitcom, complete with laugh track. One of the only ways to bring sanity to an insane situation is to hold regular, effective family meetings.

Basic Essentials

To run a functional family democratically and fairly, there must be a regular time set aside each week to discuss family issues, air feelings, and plan for the future. The family meeting is an opportunity for all members of the family to be heard on subjects that affect them directly. Just as Congress meets regularly to discuss the matters at hand for our nation, families need to meet often to organize our nation's most important institution. Family meetings are not a place where parents turn over all the authority and power to their children—that would be permissive. Within limits, parents can delegate and moderate much of the family decision making to the family members, each member having an equal voice. Examples of decisions to be made in a family meeting include:

Choosing family chores
Planning family outings and family vacations
Handling complaints and concerns
Establishing family rules and laws

Most children are thrilled to be included in family decision making. Self-esteem increases significantly as children feel capable and valued in areas they never had input before. Children can sense that parents care about the children's feelings and value their opinions. This sense of pride and responsibility carries over to peer relationships and school performance as confidence in themselves increases and family relationships are enhanced.

Occasionally, someone chooses not to attend, such as the teenager who views any form of cooperation as giving in while waging a power struggle with parents. The child who can't believe that parents now value his or her opinion when they never have before can view these meetings as futile or even manipulative. Nevertheless, the natural and logical consequence for not attending these meetings is that other family members who choose to attend will make decisions that affect the entire family, excluding input from the missing family member. A few weeks of family decision making without any say in the process prompts the self-alienated child to join the next family meeting. We've seen this happen in our own family many times. Once the perceived power struggle or control issue has passed, the child participates and never wants to miss again.

Introducing the Family Meeting

Any child who can communicate can participate in a family meeting, even the youngest of children. The initial meeting should be kept brief and the introduction simple. All family members should gather in a place appropriate for a meeting, such as the living room or family room. Beginning your family meetings in a formal way can let younger children know the importance and the responsibility connected with this process. Parents can start by stating that if they were the children again, they might feel left out in a family where the parents make all the decisions. As children, they might feel unimportant and angry about it, too. Therefore, you would like to talk with them about meeting weekly to have them take part in family decisions. When parents ask what the children think about this idea, they are usually thrilled. At this point, a time needs to be established for your family's weekly meetings. Meeting only in times of crisis will create family crises, just as talking together as a couple only in times of crisis will keep a marriage in crisis. Marriage meetings weekly are a great idea, too, as discussed in the chapter "Your Marriage Matters in Parenting."

The Casual Approach

Some family members might not respond well to a formal meeting at first. For children or spouses who might resist a formal approach to meeting, use a more casual approach to begin. For example, at dinner a family outing can be planned or ideas can be brainstormed for the week's family fun. After an outing is agreed upon, specific responsibilities for the activity can be decided and then delegated. If children do not follow through with their agreed-upon assignments, the entire family needs to experience the consequence of that choice. This drives home the point that if everyone does not pull together, the entire family suffers. Without excusing them from their duties or singling out any child for nonperformance, teamwork will be reinforced. Parents need to refrain from being dictative or detective. The child will more likely acknowledge his mistake and desire to do better if he is not punished or humiliated. Interdependence and cooperation is the family task. With the family now cooperating at some level, problems and chores can be informally introduced at subsequent, more formal meetings.

Meeting Rules

Formal governing bodies such as city councils use Robert's Rules of Order ("I second the motion") to organize and conduct meetings consistently and fairly. Familiarizing older children with Robert's Rules is not a bad idea, because they will likely encounter Robert's Rules in the future. Although we don't suggest enforcing Robert's

Rules in your home, family meetings should have some kind of ground rules by which to operate. You will begin and modify your own list as time goes on, but here's a start.

1. Meet at an agreed-upon time each week.
2. Allow all members to participate on issues as equals.
3. Agree upon the length of the meeting to avoid overwhelming or boring family members.
4. Rotate meeting responsibilities.
   - Meeting chairperson—Gives different family members the floor
   - Meeting secretary/recorder—Takes down written minutes (old and new business) and posts them following the meeting
   - Lesson chairperson—Gives short lesson or story on a topic the family could use help on that week
   - Dessert chairperson—Chooses dessert to follow the meeting
   - Dinner chairperson—Chooses the dinner on meeting day
   - Game chairperson—Chooses a family game for family members to play after the meeting
5. Plan family fun—weekly and monthly outings, yearly vacations.
6. Discuss good things that happen in the family as well as difficulties to be resolved. Work for consensus so that no one feels as though she lost an argument about a new rule or consequence. If consensus can't be reached, table the discussion for the next family meeting.
7. Use reflective listening and other skills to help all members share and pinpoint real issues. Reflective listening often helps families pinpoint the real issues and underlying emotions between what has been said and what is meant.

Pitfalls to Avoid

Here are some tips that might save headaches associated with family meetings. The family meeting process tends to not go well when the following occur.

1. Meetings are used only to handle a family crisis.
2. Parents often change meeting times or skip the meetings altogether.
3. Meetings are too long.
4. Parents dominate the meeting.
5. Decisions are not put into action.
6. Allowing discouragement to set in when consensus is often not reached quickly each time an issue is brought up. Keep discussing or just table it.
7. Only chores and complaints are discussed at the meeting.
8. Meetings are held for emergencies when not everyone agrees a meeting is necessary.

Parents need to realize that they can be the greatest hazard to a family meeting's success. It has been our experience that when parents initially use the meeting strictly for their own purposes, the children choose not to participate, feeling manipulated. All members must participate as equals for the meetings to be effective. Therefore, agenda items that involve everyone should be the ones discussed. Issues such as which suit Dad will buy or how Mom will redo the master bedroom should not be brought up. Family fun, delegation of chores, and family problems should be discussed.

Parents should set the example and be on time to meetings—your enthusiasm or lack thereof will snowball. During the week, parents should refuse to settle issues that can and should be brought up at the family meeting. A reply of "That will be a good thing to bring up at our next meeting" should do it. In our home, we have a memo pad on our refrigerator to list just such items.

Beginning a Formal Meeting

Once a date and time are established, the family meeting should take place on time, regardless of the busy lives of teenagers and parents. Anyone who chooses not to show up should not be reminded excessively. Family decisions will be made by members who attend. The decisions stand until the next family meeting. Introduce the concept of organization and planning to the family and the importance of equal voice in a family democracy. By including everyone in the meetings, all members have a sense of belonging to a family organization and being an integral part of it.

At your first meeting, establish the following procedures for your own family organization.

1. What jobs/responsibilities need to be delegated and rotated at each meeting?
2. How will we rotate job/meeting responsibilities?
3. How often should we meet as a family and for how long?
4. Will we work toward consensus or only majority rule?

Two Examples of Family Meetings

Perhaps the best way of showing how a family meeting should be run is to give a couple of examples of hypothetical family meetings.

Family One

In the first family, present at the meeting are a mother with her 15-year-old son, Craig, and with daughters Michelle, age 12, and Emily, age 6.

Mom: Even though I'm chairman of our meeting this first time, I think we should rotate the position so everyone can have a chance.

Craig: It won't matter who's chairman—you don't care what we say anyway.

Mom: You feel that this meeting is hopeless because you believe I'm unfair?

[Note that Mom has used reflective listening to pinpoint Craig's discouragement.]

Craig: Yeah, so let's do what we want and forget this dumb meeting.

Mom: It seems that you don't want to continue. But I believe a family meeting can help with organizing our family for our chores, fun, allowances, and other issues.

Last week, Craig, you said that you felt your chores were unfair and you wanted to choose them. Michelle, you mentioned that you were interested in earning some extra spending money.

Craig: Yeah ... I guess.

Mom: Michelle, are you still interested in earning extra spending money? How about you, Emily?

Michelle: Sure!

Emily: Lots!

Mom: I have a list of all the chores I could think of around the house. Can you all think of any others?

[Silence for a few moments as they look over the list.]

Craig: I'm not cleaning any toilets!

Michelle: I'm sick of doing dishes!

Emily: I'll do anything, Mom!

Craig: That's just like Miss Goody-Goody—Kiss up to everyone!

Mom: I don't think we will get anywhere with name calling and we can't continue if we do. Craig, if you choose to name call and leave the meeting, I guess we can choose your jobs for you, but we would rather have your input.

Craig: I'm sorry, Emily *[brief pause]* but I still *refuse* to clean toilets or do dishes!

Mom: Why would it be fair for you not to do the unpleasant jobs, while everyone else has to take their turn? Does that seem fair to you?

Craig: I guess not.

Mom: OK, now, who has an idea of how to pick our chores?

[As first chairperson, Mom is helping everyone stay on task to keep the meeting flowing and within the time allotted.]

Michelle: Why don't we take turns choosing from the list?

Craig: Yeah—oldest first.

Emily: No! Youngest!

Mom: So far, Michelle has suggested we each take turns

choosing jobs from the list. Are there any other ideas?
[*Mom stays on task, thus avoiding another argument. After brief silence, Mom continues.*]

Mom: Is everyone in favor of taking turns choosing until the list is filled?
[*Everyone nods affirmatively.*]

We have had two suggestions on deciding the order of choosing. Craig suggested the oldest choose first and Emily suggested that the youngest choose first. Are there any other ideas?

Emily: We could choose numbers like at school. I could make the four papers and put them in a bowl.
[*After everyone agrees that is the fairest way, the chores are chosen and Mom continues.*]

Mom: As before, allowances will be given when jobs are completed on time and without nagging. Is that fair?

Michelle: Even with allowance, I still need more money to do things I want, because there isn't much baby-sitting these days.

Mom: Michelle, do you have any other ideas on how to earn more money?
[*Silence.*]

Mom: Does anyone else?

Craig: You could get a paper route like me.

Michelle: Yuck!

Mom: I appreciate your desire to help our family, Craig. I don't feel comfortable giving my suggestions, Michelle, if they will get comments like Craig's received.
[*Mom used an "I" statement to express her frustration and her refusal to help if criticized also.*]

Michelle: Sorry, Craig, I just hate getting up early. Mom, what's your idea?

Mom: I could make an extra list of seasonal/one time jobs with dollar values that you or anyone can choose from when you need extra money for things.

Many families find it helpful to have some form of time card/chart system for their children to record finished jobs. This eliminates reminders and nagging. Parents assume that children can do the things they want to do when they have shown they have completed the things that they needed to do. Children are not eligible to earn extra money elsewhere or at home until they have fulfilled their current home chore obligations. Here is an example of an accountability card that could be devised at a family meeting.

Each family member's card differs according to the jobs chosen during a particular time period. Some agreed-upon work rules are also written on the charts for quick reference—TV off at 9:30 on Saturdays, for example. Charts for younger children can have pictures instead of words. Many software programs available today provide artwork that can be easily cut and pasted onto such charts.

Family Two

Excerpts from a meeting already in progress with a younger family. Mom and Dad with four younger children: Tyler (11), Cameron (9), Andrea (6), and Mindy (4).

Tyler (Meeting chairperson): OK, Dad, did you want to say something?
Dad: I just wanted to thank Andrea for reading that book about the Berenstain Bears' politeness plan. They had some good ideas for keeping manners in their home. I wish we could establish a plan in our own home.
Andrea: We could!
Cameron: Be quiet, Andrea. Do you want more jobs and work around here?
Mom: Cameron, it sounds like you don't like the idea.
Cameron: I like things the way they are.
Mom: Does anyone have anything they would change?
[Mindy raises her hand.]
Tyler: Mindy, what bugs you?
Mindy: Cameron yelling at me.

Job Chart for Older Child

Daily Jobs	Mon	Tues	Wed	Thurs	Fri	Sat	Sun
Homework							
Practice							
Sweeping							
Own bathroom							
Bedroom							
Clear table							
Dishwasher							
Citizenship							

Saturday Jobs

Vacuum room	
Vacuum hall	
Clean under bed	
Clean closet	
Vacuum stairs	
Mop floor	
Sort socks	

-$1 per day, $6 per week
-$4 bonus, if no reminders or fines
-Rest OK, but no TV or play until don
-If goof off, no snack time next day
    plus extra job
-No pay until Saturday jobs done
-TV off at 9:30 on Saturday

Job Chart for Younger Child

Jobs		Mon	Tues	Wed	Thurs	Fri	Sat	Sun
	[Make your bed}							
	[Feed cat]							
	[Feed turtle]							
	[Get the mail]							
	[Water plants]							
	[Citizenship]							

Dad: How does everyone feel about yelling in the home?

Mom: It makes me feel very uncomfortable and on edge. I wish it would stop.

Tyler: Mom, what's your idea to stop it?

Mom: I guess I'd like everyone else's input before I jump in.

Mindy: Let's have a time-out place for people who yell.

Mom: That's a great start, Mindy!

Tyler: Any other ideas?

Dad: I think noise would be best kept outside.

Tyler: How about staying outside on time-out until you're ready to come back in with a quiet voice?

[Everyone nods approval; Andrea raises her hand.]

What, Andrea?

Andrea: At school, if we yell again we stay out in the hall until the teacher is ready for us to come back. At home, we could wait until Mom and Dad invite us back in.

The family continues discussing the following issues, which will be added to the family's personal politeness plan.

Interrupting: If someone interrupts another family member who is talking to someone else or who is on the phone, the offender cleans that person's room or if the room is already clean, does another job for that person.

Slamming doors: $1 fine for each offense.

Table manners violation: Resume eating after five-minute time-out period (can choose to wait in room or on couch).

All family members sign the rules, which will remain in force after being written in the family book by Cameron, the recorder. After their thirty-minute meeting, everyone enjoys frozen yogurt chosen by Mindy, the refreshment chairperson for the meeting.

It's crucial to learn how to run a successful family meeting before you implement one. The patterns demonstrated above can help. Remember the concept of representative voice as the rule, not the exception. All decisions made in meetings should stand until changed or amended in subsequent meetings. It is even helpful to have family members sign minutes when laws and consequences have been established and consensus has been reached. This avoids any "I don't remember agreeing to that" later on.

All family members are subject to the laws and to the consequences for breaking those laws at the family meetings. In our own home, even we parents have spent time-out for breaking rules and have had to miss out on dessert on a few occasions. It is important for children to see that their parents don't receive preferential treatment under the rules, as dictators would.

Regardless of your family situation, regular family meetings are crucial. It's important to *never* give up once you begin this process, despite the attempts of any family members to discourage you. Your first few meetings might be disasters, but naturally you will get better with practice. In just a few months of weekly meetings, your family will have developed a great long-lasting tradition.

Family meetings are an essential step in helping families help themselves. Families can be self-correcting only if they establish regular family meetings. They will create unity and love in the home, heal resentments, and avoid the serious family problems that psychologists and therapists all over the country deal with on a daily basis.

Twelve

Blended Families: Step-Success

In 1970, 69 percent of all marriages were the first for both the bride and the groom. Today, less than half are. The stepfamily might soon be the most prevalent type of family, deserving increased attention on family and parenting issues. Unfortunately, the divorce rate in second marriages is even higher than in first-time unions—about 70 percent versus 50 percent—and is highest of all when children are involved in blended families—about 80 percent.

These statistics indicate that blended families face challenges that first-marriage families do not. In addition to obvious ex-spousal and financial issues, the relationships in blended families are more complex because there are usually more people affected. Blended family members are required to adjust quickly to new relationships that are intensely personal: parents, children, and siblings. Interacting with one another takes time—some professionals feel it takes an average of five years for a blended family to truly blend.

Having worked with blended families and children of divorced parents for more than a decade, Kimberly has witnessed the anger that develops in children after a divorce. Often unaware of the abrupt changes occurring with their parents, children resent the upheaval and insecurity thrust on them obviously without their consent.

Children of divorce, as many stepparents know, sometimes try to sabotage the new relationship by refusing to share their biological parent. Going back and forth between parents in what we call the yo-yo effect creates further resentment in children and severe guilt for the parents involved. Parental guilt can result in each spouse putting his or her own children's interests before the other spouse and the other spouse's children—a perfect formula for disaster.

So what is the formula for success? In addition to the skills already discussed in this book, there are six keys to creating a functional stepfamily.

1. Strengthen the Marital Union

As stated in the chapter "Your Marriage Matters in Parenting," strengthening any marriage boosts parenting effectiveness. However, paying attention to your marriage is especially important when combining families because all forces are usually present to pull the union apart. Parenting challenges are tough enough on a first-time family. When the challenges involve stepparents or stepchildren, the marital discord is amplified exponentially. During the first few months, marriage meetings—every day if necessary—are important for finding ways of keeping love alive in the relationship and establishing unified ground rules for parenting. Weekly fun in the form of spouse date nights is especially important for the newly created spousal union for two reasons. First, by allowing the couple to spend needed time together, their new marriage relationship solidifies. Second, by allowing children to observe their parents going out together, establishing their new bond, the new marriage gains credibility and engenders the requisite respect from the children for the newly established all-important relationship.

Kimberly relates:
Phil and Nancy came to treatment in their golden years having been married only two years following the death of both of their spouses. They were experiencing marital discord largely because of issues related to their two married

children—one from each spouse. Both of their children placed demands on their parent for babysitting, maintaining their homes, and even financial support. These pressures were so intense that the elderly couple were being pulled apart in the process of trying to serve their children. During the first session, we discussed establishing time for their relationship apart from their married children. Date nights were again established as was special time—sacred hours—each day that no child's phone call could interrupt. Phil and Nancy were amazed how easily this was established and respected by their children once implemented.

Problems and parenting issues that arise in a newly blended family should be discussed first by the parents from each viewpoint. Each spouse complements the other because of the different perspectives they bring to the marriage. They should be able to state the other spouse's view before discussing solutions and deciding upon one. Understanding each other is key to good compromising. Brainstorming all possible solutions before making decisions ultimately leads to a better decision. It is important to table all decisions until consensus between spouses is reached.

Kimberly relates:

Dorothy came to treatment alone with her 16-year-old son for their first session, complaining of his lack of respect for the law. He had been caught shoplifting, and Dorothy felt that this was because of his pain from the divorce from her husband three years earlier. She mentioned that she didn't bring her second husband with her because the husband felt her son should go to jail for what he had done. She stated that she and her husband could not agree on what to do. The second meeting was spent with the couple only, without the son, discussing their differences and how together they have the makings for wonderful discipline. Dorothy had experienced trouble setting limits with her son. Interestingly, this was actually one of the things that subconsciously attracted her to her second husband—his ability to discipline and actually follow through with necessary consequences. He, on the other hand, was attracted to Dorothy's nurturing qualities and her ability to see things from the other person's perspective. The meeting proved insightful as each looked at their differences in a positive way and used them to work out the challenges with their son.

To reach a consensus for parenting a blended family, both husband and wife must discuss all problems and parenting issues from both perspectives. There are so many loyalty issues with each parent's own biological kids that need to be worked through. Although child loyalty probably causes the most discord in remarriages, there are many other issues.

- Relationships with ex-spouses and the effect of those relationships on the children as they go back and forth between parents for visitation
- Financial issues, such as child support or alimony payments
- Personal modesty issues, which for most blended families are surprisingly important. Should behaviors differ in the newly formed stepfamily? Can the young children still be allowed into their parents' bed? Should one or both parents, or teen children, be allowed to roam in their underwear, as they previously were accustomed to doing, in full view of new family members?

All of these potential areas of discord in blended families must be worked out together. Brainstorm all possible solutions before deciding. Table all decisions until consensus is reached. This is accomplished through successful family meetings, which is the next step. However, couples must meet beforehand without the children to help channel discussions in appropriate ways with ideas of how these issues can be resolved successfully. Without preplanning, family meetings could potentially result in chaos.

2. Establish Weekly Family Meetings

Initial family meetings are helpful for the newly formed stepfamily to learn to merely communicate with new family members. Family meetings also help children mourn the loss of their other family. This is a universal issue for stepfamilies that must be addressed. A child often feels torn between the parent he lives with and the divorced parent who lives somewhere else. As discussion leaders, both parents can calmly encourage other family members to empathize with the sad child, who is probably not alone in such feelings if there are other children in the blended family. Other children, whether of the same parent or not, are probably feeling the same thing. When such challenges are faced creatively through family meetings, members of the blended family can build strong new bonds among themselves.

During meetings, family members can learn to express their own personal feelings, goals, dreams, and thoughts. They can also learn to support each other. Family meetings can foster new skills for making decisions as a family and working toward consensus. A good way of learning to achieve consensus in a blended family is planning weekly family fun together. Ideas from the past and new ideas can be combined to establish new traditions necessary for a blended family's success. Learning to reach consensus on relatively less important issues, such as family recreation, can lay the groundwork for effectively resolving much more weighty issues in the future.

Kimberly relates:
The Smith-Jones family used family meetings in their home immediately after practicing together for the first time in my office. They had many issues to deal with as a newly formed family with four children (two from each spouse). Visitation schedules were the first order of business as family members tried to schedule family togetherness time around weekend and midweek visits. A definite time for future family meetings was decided on, and the mechanism was in place for dealing with the many other issues that would arise in this blended family's future.

3. Establish Family Tradition

A family tradition is considered any event that occurs with regularity and holds special meaning for a family or individual family members. Holiday traditions may involve special food preparation, treats to neighbors, or favorite house decorations. Family traditions of whatever type, even spring cleaning, can create feelings of warmth, closeness, continuity, and cohesiveness in what seems to a child to be a world of chaos. Newly established traditions can give special meaning to a child that helps him face the challenges he'll encounter each new day. Blended families can decide in their family meetings which traditions to keep. It is also important for the family's cohesiveness to add new traditions of their own.

Each family member could come to the meeting with a list of activities that all stepfamily members would enjoy. Ideas could range from visiting a national park each year to having a special reading hour prior to bedtime each night, with parents taking turns reading from a favorite book. Establishing weekly family meetings in and of itself can be one of the best family traditions for blended families. The meeting should provide an emotionally safe, nonconfrontational environment for all members to vent their feelings appropriately in the presence of mutual respect. Once a family tradition is established, someone in the family should write it down in a journal or a calendar so that it can happen in the future. This allows repetition, thus establishing and defining a tradition.

We know one blended family who decided in one of their first family meetings to go camping for a week each summer around visitation schedules. Every spring, family members suggested where the family wanted to camp, and a family vote determined the majority's interest that summer. This family found that camping was a perfect family tradition, which helped its members work and play together in a neutral and fun environment. Camping also provided many opportunities for creatively solving problems and bonding through work.

4. Deal with a Stepchild's Rebellion

Rebellion of stepchildren happens all too often, mostly as a result of parental guilt—"If I had only kept the marriage together, Johnny wouldn't be acting up." While it is true that a child's emotional security is disrupted for a time, not everything that happens can or should be blamed on a split in a family. Often the divorce is a reason for negative behavior and rebellion but is no excuse for it. Parents need to deal with rebellion immediately when it surfaces, identifying why it is counterproductive and how the emotional display can be better expressed. Family meetings are a perfect place to set natural and logical consequences for negative behaviors before they become a problem. The longer these behaviors continue, the harder they are to stop. Parents need to deal with their own issues of guilt or extenuating circumstances that make necessary consequences for negative behaviors difficult to implement.

> Kimberly relates:
>
> Sixteen-year-old Doug began treatment after his mother was desperate for help with his escalating negative behaviors. His mother had divorced Doug's father nearly twelve years earlier but failed to discipline him or allow his stepfather of ten years to discipline Doug, fearing it would result in emotional trauma to Doug and his 14-year-old brother, Jeff. Three years previously, the mother had taken both boys to their pediatrician with many of the same behaviors, and the doctor put both boys on Ritalin. Now older teenagers with their behaviors worsening—even on higher doses of medication—the mother didn't know where to turn.
>
> We initially discussed that although divorce can instigate negative behaviors in children initially, these behaviors should not be excused because of the divorce. They had merely become bad habits, which needed to be stopped. We set up a plan to do just that, which included natural and

*logical consequences for each destructive behavior, marriage
meetings, and family meetings to evaluate progress and work
toward blended family harmony. Although such a plan
when implemented works well with most families, Doug's
mother would not follow through with any consequences she
and her husband had set up because she felt she had inflict-
ed enough trauma on the boys with the divorce from their
father. Because their natural father spent no time with the
boys, she felt consequences would be interpreted by the boys
as further rejection, added to those they had suffered from
their father already. Sadly, the behaviors intensified with no
limits, and the oldest boy had to be placed outside the home.
The guilt she felt from her divorce caused her to overindulge
her sons, which in turn caused the boys to become manipulative and disobedient, taking a tremendous toll on her second marriage. Putting her sons' interests first and her husband's somewhere down the list was a formula for marital
disaster. After her oldest son's placement, she was more willing to look at these family dynamics and the guilt she was
feeling.*

Another case example:

*Elizabeth brought her 14-year-old daughter, Megan, to
treatment, fearing that she had deep-rooted anger about the
divorce of her mother and father three years earlier.
Elizabeth further explained that her concerns stemmed from
Megan's frequent refusals to go to school, complaining of
stomach aches. During the most recent episode, Megan was
home for nearly a month. I noticed that Megan was very
manipulative when we met in session. It was obvious to me
that Elizabeth catered to Megan's every whim, to her detriment. When we discussed a plan to get her daughter back in
school, Elizabeth hesitated at first, stating that the divorce*

*had been traumatic and the father's lack of parental involve-
ment was also hard on her daughter. Although children can
have delayed grief reactions to divorce and can experience
depression from parental abandonment, I did not believe
this to be the case with Megan, a very smug and manipulative child.*

*As we explored the situation further, Elizabeth realized
that she had allowed herself to be manipulated largely
because of her fear that if held more accountable for school,
her daughter would change her mind and choose to live with
her father in retaliation. Although granted full custody of
her daughter, Elizabeth's fear was causing her to be manipulated to the detriment of her daughter's functional future
and her own as well.*

5. Keep the Children out of the Middle

When children are put in the middle of feuding ex-spouses, nobody
wins, but the children lose the most. Still loyal to both parents, children's dual alliance can cause mental and emotional strain. The children feel somehow guilty for the divorce. They also feel the stress of
their powerlessness to fix the situation. Most divorced couples can
figure this out on their own, but children are put between fighting
parents all too often, from hate or selfishness of the parents—either
consciously or unconsciously. Unconsciously, ex-spouses want
revenge so badly, they forget that the child they love will suffer far
more than the real target of their hate. On the other hand, incredible
as it seems, parents sometimes consciously try to damage their children as the ultimate weapon against their ex-spouse. We believe that
parents who try to hurt their exes, even if their own innocent children get caught in the middle, are the worst humankind has to offer.
They really never grew up themselves.

Adults should always deal directly with other adults involved.
The best guideline is to remind all adult parties that each parent

should try to keep the best interest of the child at heart. Sadly, children often put themselves in the middle, hoping to mend the most significant third-party relationship in their lives—the relationship between their parents. Responsible parents, divorce notwithstanding, should put a stop to this, which is not a child's job nor function. All adults involved, custodial and noncustodial parents as well as relatives and friends, should cooperate for the good of the children, which means that you should not only keep children out of the middle of adult communications, but you should also be as amenable as possible to each other. If ex-spouses feud bitterly, children pick up on the acrimony and inevitably start to feel guilty all over again.

Kimberly relates:

Jane, age 40, was referred by her doctor to my office for treatment for recurrent depression and anxiety attacks. When we discussed the issues she was dealing with, she focused mostly on the age of her boys—they were leaving the nest soon. Though most parents experience loss when their children leave, this is heightened for individuals who have invested solely in their children, ignoring the marriage relationship. However, Jane had a strong marriage and her husband was very supportive. Further discussion revealed an extremely hostile relationship between her own mother and father during their divorce when Jane was 12 years old. Both parents went to war with each other and placed their children on the front lines. They manipulated the children by using the court system and made the children reject the other parent. Also, after the children were split up to live with one parent or the other, the children were not allowed to contact the other parent, which was not court ordered. Jane was devastated to lose a nurturing, supportive parent she loved so dearly. Her panic attacks and depression were projected from her greatest loss as a child onto the perceived impending loss of her sons as they prepared to enter adulthood.

Most people would probably agree that, in general, new TV shows and movies are not particularly family friendly, with the usual suspects to blame: sex and violence—not to mention the cutting and sarcastic way family members treat each other. However, we think that one positive thing Hollywood has done of late is to portray in a positive light the dealings of divorced parents with each other on visitations and other issues. This is not the norm, though we wish it could be.

6. Focus on Strengths

It is true that blended families have a wider network of extended family than first marriages. Children benefit from having more relatives to interact with and draw strength from. There are often more opportunities for sharing experiences, hobbies, and interests that are seemingly endless and available to a newly blended family. Children also don't ignore the extra presents that come during any given holiday or birthday.

Strong blended families often value commitment even more than first-marriage families, having experienced the result when commitment breaks down. They also value the characteristics that make their new family unique. The new marriage union creates a second chance for happiness and therefore commits the couple even more strongly to each other than they were to their previous spouse. Realizing mistakes from the past, parents often resolve to make it work this time no matter what. Getting old enough to see friends divorce, we notice how their behavior toward marriage can change— they seem more serious than ever to make their marriages work. Typically, the parental adults in blended families tend to be older, which may mean they are more mature and have learned from divorce, one of life's toughest experiences. If difficulties arise in the new marriage or family, they are often wise enough and committed enough to take a step back and redouble their efforts, even seeking counseling from a therapist, their clergy, or a support group, something they never would have considered before. Remarried adults know firsthand the consequences of poor communication and spouse neglect and are often more motivated than first-marriage adults.

By following these steps, many blended families have beaten the odds and have created wonderful new marriages and family relationships. Success is possible if you take the time to nurture and strengthen these relationships. His and hers can definitely become ours, with time and effort.

Conclusion

Taking Down the Scaffolding

W e wrote this book only so that we could share what we've learned through our own experience and the experience of others. Really good parenting is difficult; it is tough work that each and every day requires gritty tenacity, just as any other of life's battles. It is not any easier for us than for you. In fact, it's probably tougher for us by virtue of sheer numbers. We have six wonderful children and want every single one of them to grow up to be wonderful adults—any parent's wish. Achieving that in our house, as in yours, no matter what your family size, takes daily, consistent effort. We can tell you, however, that applying the principles in this book does make the job of parenting easier, although breaking old patterns is initially difficult.

We want to share our thoughts with you on the importance of having a stay-at-home parent—not always the mother these days—to raise children in their formative years. Like ADD, this is a controversial and personal topic on which not everyone will agree. As with other views stated in this book, these opinions are ours to express and yours to adopt or discard. We do not feel we are alone in our views, but realize that an opposing viewpoint is legitimately held by intelligent, caring people.

In 1997, 64 percent of women with children under 6 worked full time, up from 30 percent in 1970 and only 18 percent in 1960. This trend has produced dramatic changes in our society, some of which are dysfunctional. Certainly, the expanded career opportunities for women in recent decades is, in general, a positive development, especially for financial independence for a woman trying to escape an abusive marriage or provide for her family upon the death or divorce of her husband who was the primary breadwinner. We have encouraged and will continue to encourage our own daughters to get all the education possible. We didn't write the rules, but the rules of the world seem to be that education is the key to a good life and a broad horizon of options. We want all of our children to have the flexibility and independence that a good education provides.

We fully acknowledge that sometimes being a full-time working mother is simply unavoidable. We also know that limited part-time work can be enriching. Kimberly's practice keeps her professional skills active until the kids are grown, when she would like to explore more options. However, parents need to know how much is too much and set limits on themselves. Failure to do so usually springs from a perceived and artificial need for more income, the human appetite, which is naturally infinite. We have found that kids really do enjoy gifts from Toys-R-Us just as much as from FAO Schwartz, and that the weekend house at the beach is not one of life's necessities. The I-have-to-work refrain, with a sigh from the young mother married to a high-power, high-income type who drives away from the day care center in her new BMW, rings a bit hollow to us.

The *Wall Street Journal* reports that in 1997, employees said they spend about three hours of a given workday on child-related tasks. If both parents work full time in demanding jobs, those three hours (somewhat high in many cases) probably overlap. Who is parenting during the other thirteen hours of the day the child is awake? Our point is that mothers and fathers with school-aged children who both work long hours outside the home often do so at a significant cost to their children. Studies debate the effects of nonfamily care on children, let alone the sensationalized stories in the media of child neglect or even abuse under such care. We realize that the vast majority of day care centers are not abusive, and many day care situations work fine for all parties concerned. Granted, a grandma can be the perfect answer, but even grandmas often need their own lives. As for us, however, we have chosen careers that allow a parent to be home with the children at all times. We made that decision long before another *Wall Street Journal* article reported that a stay-at-home parent is a new luxury of the modern age. Our lifestyle is far from luxurious, but we found that nobody really cares for your child the way you, the parent, do. Granted, by the time children turn 4 or 5, they are ready for the outside world, that is, preschool or kindergarten— and the parents are *ready* for them to be ready. However, parents should be, whenever humanly possible, at the crossroads, which generally are not the monumental decisions of college, career, and marriage, but rather the daily, simple talks at the kitchen table when children come home from school. Long workweeks and extended business travel by both the mother and father of young children who are in day care ten or twelve hours a day place a healthy, functional family life at risk, we believe. Dozens and dozens of sad instances from Kimberly's practice bear this out. You can have most of it, but you can't have it all.

When the time comes to take down the parenting scaffolding as children go off to college or otherwise leave the nest, you hope to see a marvelous building constructed in the form of adult children who are responsible, caring, contributing members of society and their own families. A friend of ours has another analogy for winding down the parenting job: the Jell-O mold. When it's time to remove the mold, you never know if the Jell-O will have set sufficiently to stand on its own.

We think the chances dramatically improve with the level of effort expended to create a functional, democratically run family. It's not easy, but it's worth it—the potential rewards are huge. Imagine yourself visiting in the home of one your grown children who has married and started a family of his own some years from now. Among your grandchildren, it is clear that feelings are respected. "I" statements send appropriate communication without belittling and yelling. It appears that the children respect each other and their parents, who deal with misbehavior in ways that follow rules apparently set up in advance. "We'll talk about that in our next family meeting" is a phrase you hear, a seeming echo of the words you used at one time to maintain order in the home, another example of which you see before you. Reflective listening is the rule. It is then you realize that the struggle to implement democracy in your home many years ago paid off.

A paycheck from a job in the working world comes regularly. The paycheck for parenting may come sporadically, or in some cases, not at all. But when the honest work of parenting is invested, the paycheck can come with more abundance and happiness than from any job. And the rewards keep coming. When you retire from your job, unless your name is on the front of the building, few people will really know or care what you did there, in all honesty. What counts is the reason you went to work—to support your family. Success in one's career is fulfilling and important, but people sometimes fail to keep it in perspective. Few executives have died with the words on their lips, "I just wish I had spent more time at the office."

We can think of few things more rewarding than knowing we have left a legacy of healthy parenting. Whereas biological evolution is slow, emotional change can occur quickly in a family line, bringing a completely different situation to a home. That depends on the choices that the parents make, and of course, the choices the children make in response to the environment set up by the parents. The point is, the future of your family can be written by you. If you apply the principles in this book, although not always easy, we hope you will find the payoff in family harmony and unity that functional families enjoy despite the dysfunctional world around them.

SUGGESTED READINGS

Adler, Alfred. *What Life Should Mean to You*. New York: G.P. Putnam's Sons, 1958.

Dinkmeyer, D., and G. McKay. *Raising a Responsible Child*. New York: Simon and Schuster, 1973.

Dreikurs, Rudolph, and V. Soltz. *Children: The Challenge*. New York: Hawthorn Books, Inc., 1964.

Covey, Stephen R. *7 Habits of Highly Effective Families*. New York: Simon and Schuster, 1998.

Eyre, Linda and Richard. *Teaching Your Children Values*. New York: Simon and Schuster, 1993.

Lund, John L. *Avoiding Emotional Divorce*. Orem, UT: Noble Publishing, Inc., 1982.

Nelsen, Jane. *Positive Discipline*. New York: Ballantine Books, 1987.

NOTES

p. 26 *Fifty-six percent* ed. J. Heslop, (1997), *The American Marketplace: Demographics and Spending Patterns.* 3d ed. Ithaca, NY: Strategist.

p. 88 *As early as 1918* Adler, A. (1964), *Social Interest.* New York: Capricorn Books.

p. 227 *Prescriptions for Ritalin* Gibbs, N. (1998), "The Age of Ritalin," *Time,* December 30, 86–96.

Index

A

accountability, 149–51
Adler, Alfred, 61
adolescents
  attitudes, ix
  bedtime, 141–42
  college costs, 13–14
  and consequences, 113
  curfews, 8, 29–30
  driving, 7–8, 113
  financial responsibility, 11
  hormones, 146–47
  in Japan, 68
  rebelliousness, 80
alcohol, 98–99
alimony, 173
allowances, 8, 9–10, 137–39. *See also*
  financial responsibility
anxiety, 88–89, 155
Arnstein, 61
assertiveness, 98
Attention Deficit Disorder (ADD), 38,
  145–49, 155–57
Attention Deficit Hyperactivity Disorder
  (ADHD). *See* Attention Deficit
  Disorder
attention-seeking
  and birth order, 56–57, 62
  as misbehavior cause, 26–28, 36
  night fears, 141
  parental response, 28–29, 34, 57
authorities, threats to call, 93
autocratic parenting
  and Attention Deficit Disorder, 154
  child motivating techniques, 66
  communication example, 81
  definition, 1
  and discouragement, 37
  and household chores, 135

  and neatness, 95
  pendulum effect, 45–46
  and problem ownership, 95, 96

B

bedtime, 8, 74, 140–42
bed wetting, 153
birth order
  firstborn, 35, 54–59
  middle child, 60–61
  only child, 63
  second child, 59–60
  youngest child, 61–63
blended families. *See also under* parenting
  benefits, 180–81
  establishing traditions, 175
  ex-spouses, 173, 178
  family meetings, 174
  modesty issues, 173
  parenting consensus, 172–73
  visitation schedules, 174
boredom, 151
bullies, 88–89, 96–97

C

chauffeuring, 119, 130
cheating, 98
children. *See also* special children
  and crises, 15–17
  discouragement feelings, 32–39
  of divorced parents, x, 37–39, 155, 176–79
  and expectations of others, 61, 76
  nature *versus* nurture, 21–22
  needs *versus* wants, 10, 36
  and parental marriage relationship, 48
  and problem ownership, 96–105
  respect for, 76
  stages and behavior, 22–25
chores

assigning, 118–19, 135–37
and consequences, 121, 135–39
and driving, 113
and home common areas, 95
job charts, 167
payment, 7–10, 12–13, 137–39
performance quality, 117, 139
classroom violence, 99–100
college costs, 13–14
communication
in family meetings, 161
feeling about because (FAB), 83–85
"I" statements, 80, 85
negative, 79–80
nonverbal, 83, 95
parent to teacher, 87–88
problem-solving steps, 85–87
response examples, 81–82
competition, 59–60, 68–70, 72
conflict resolution, 104–5
consequences. *See also* order
and bedtime, 140–42
description, 107–9
for different children, 119
of disrespect for parents, 142–43
effectiveness, 109–11
enforcement, 122–23
and household chores, 135–39
and morning routine, 128–31
for parents, 169
and school work, 112, 131–35, 148–50
tips for using, 122–23, 124–26, 128
and young children, 112–13
Cowen, Emory, 61
credit cards, 11
crises, 14–17, 37–39
criticism
of children, 34, 65, 79, 81
of parenting style, 116
curfews, 8, 29–30, 141–42

D
danger, 107–8, 112
dating, for parents, 49–50
decision-making. *See also* family meetings
autocratic parenting effect, 37
parental involvement, 75, 76–77, 119–20
steps, 85–87
democratic parenting, 5–7, 66. *See also* consequences; family meetings
demographic trends, ix–x

depression, 152, 153
dethronement
of father, 57
of firstborn, 35, 54–55
dinner table, 74, 95, 131, 168
discipline. *See also* consequences; punishment; structure deficit
consistency, 18–19, 37, 45–46, 110
essay approach, 24–25
and love, 73
parental consensus, 41–42, 45
discouragement
causes, 36–37
and divorce, 37–39
handling, 70–71, 114–15
and misbehavior, 35–36
of second born, 59
disrespect, 142–43
disruptive behavior, 125, 168
divorce, x, 37–39, 155, 170–71. *See also under* parenting
door slamming, 168
dressing, 66–67, 120–22. *See also* morning routine
driving, 7, 11, 113. *See also* chauffeuring
drugs, 98–99

E
eating disorders, 31–32, 36
education. *See* college costs; extracurricular activities; grades; homework; underachievement
empathy, 118
encopretic behavior, 153
encouragement
for effort, 76, 114–15
and love, 67–68, 76, 77
versus praise, 68–71
recommended phrases, 70–71
enuretic behavior, 153
extracurricular activities, 102, 111–12, 119, 148

F
fairness, 60
family meetings
attendance, 159, 162
benefits, 6
for blended families, 174
chairmanship, 59
and communication, 161

and crises, 15
and decisions, 159, 169
examples, 163–69
ground rules, 160–61, 163
and household chores, 135–37
introduction, 159–60
pitfalls, 161–62
and social order, 114
feeling about because (FAB), 83–85
financial responsibility, 9–14, 134, 137–39
firstborn child, 35, 54–59
forgetfulness, 92–93, 129
fun, 77–78

G
Gallagher, R. J., 61
grades
    and car insurance, 11
    and college costs, 13–14
    consequence approach, 112, 131–35,
        148–50
    and problem ownership, 101–3
grandparents, 116
gratitude, 74–75
grounding, 141
guilt, 38, 118, 171, 176–77

H
Hallowell, Edward, 151
handicapped children. *See* special children
heredity, 21–22
homework, 101, 114, 116–17, 131–32
humor, 75–76

I
identity, 60
illness, 14, 28–29, 33, 36
improvement, recognition of, 76
inadequacy feelings, 32–34, 59
interrupting, 168
"I" statements, 80, 85

L
labeling, 32–33, 35, 61, 149–50
limits, 91–93, 152–55
loud music, 92–93
love, 67, 71, 73–78
lunches, 92–93, 129
Lund, John, 65

M
manipulative behavior, 93, 118, 176–78
manners, 166–68
marriage
    discord and problem child, 45–46
    distance and children, 46–52
    division after first child, 44–45
    premarital counseling, 40–41
    and romance, 49–50
marriage meetings, 50–52, 171–73
meals, 92–93, 95, 131, 168. *See also* dinner
    table
meetings. *See* family meetings; marriage
    meetings
middle child, 60–61
misbehavior. *See also* attention-seeking
    cause, 35–37
    at dinner table, 95
    disruption, 125, 168
    and divorce, 37–39, 176–78
    and emotions, 84–85
    and hormones, 146–47
    and love, 67
    physical aggression, 23
    power-seeking, 29–30, 36, 62
    responsibility-dodging, 32–34
    and revenge, 30–31, 91–92
modesty issues, 173
morning routine, 128–31, 141–42
motivating techniques, 66
multiple births, 42–44
Munsch, Robert, 73

N
nature *versus* nurture, 21–22
neatness, 6, 95
needs *versus* wants, 10, 36, 151–52
negotiation skills, 84
nightmares, 88–89, 141

O
only children, 63
order, maintaining, 113–26
overachievers, 62–63
overindulgence, 35, 36, 119, 177

P
parenting. *See also* marriage
    and attention-seeking behavior, 28–29,
        34, 57

for discouraged children, 35–39
by divorced parents, 39, 176–80 (*see also*
 blended families)
and example setting, 75
expectations, 61, 76
and family meeting rules, 169
hyperactive, 150–51
and limits, 91–93
and marriage relationship, 44–48
power-assertive, 80
and power-seeking, 30, 34, 119–20
and problem-ownership, 94–96
and responsibility dodging, 32–34
and revenge, 32, 34, 91–92
showing love, 73–78
styles of (*see* autocratic parenting; democratic parenting; permissive
 parenting)
training, 2–4
and work outside home, 36, 182–85
peers, 96–100
penalties, 7–9
permissive parenting
and Attention Deficit Disorder, 152–55
definition, 1–2
and dinner table behavior, 95
and discouragement, 36–37
and neatness, 95
overinvolvement, 90–92
pendulum effect, 45–46
and refusal to do chores, 119
physical aggression, 23, 88, 105. *See also*
 violence
pity, 118
potty training, 55–56, 113, 153–54
power, 29–30, 36, 62, 119–20
praise, 68–71
pregnancy, ix, 32
priorities
for children, 12–13
of marriage relationship, 48
for time allocation, 73–74
privileges, 7–9, 55–56, 148
problem ownership, 94–105, 116–17
problem-solving, 85–86
punishment, 107, 108–9, 131, 154

R
Ratey, John, 151
Reid, Robert, 146

respect, 76, 80, 95–96, 114. *See also* disrespect
responsibility. *See also* accountability;
 problem ownership
avoidance, 32–34
for belongings, 9
for decisions, 119–20
financial, 9–14
for forgotten lunches, 92–93
and permissive parenting, 90–91
and privileges, 7–8
with siblings, 58–59, 123–24
for tasks, 114–15
rewards, 107, 131
Ritalin, 146, 154
room cleaning, 6
rules, 7, 19, 37
for family meetings, 160–61, 163

S
safety, 107–8, 112
school avoidance, 33, 88–89, 130, 177–78
security deficit, 155
self-concept, 68
self-confidence, 76, 117
self-discipline, 151–52
self-esteem, 33, 60, 69
self-image, 80, 81, 115
self-mutilation, 35
shoplifting, 91–92, 172
siblings. *See also* birth order
bonding with new baby, 54–55
caretaker approach, 63–64
and competition, 59–60, 72
and problem ownership, 104–5
relationship between, xi
and responsibility, 58–59, 123–24
and social time-out, 143
sickness, 14
Silver, Larry, 155
single parent families, x, 42, 45–46
smoking, 98–99
social order, 114
soiling underwear, 153
special children, 33, 115
sports, 69, 102
stepchildren, 176–78
stimulation deficit, 151
structure deficit, 152–55
suicide, 35, 56–57, 68

T

tantrums, 29, 115
tattling, 72
teachers, 24, 87–88, 100–101, 145–46
teasing, 97–98
time allocation, 73–74, 77–78
time-outs, 142, 143, 169
timing, 117
Toman, Walter, 63
traditions, 175
training, 117
trust, 76

U

underachievement
    versus attention deficit, 147–48
    and birth order, 59, 61
    causes, 103–4, 147–55

V

vacations, 175
violence, 99–100

W

working parents, 36, 182–85